NEW KNITTING
Fast, Fun & Easy

Florence Temko

HPBooks®

Cover photo—Left: Burgundy and metallic gold Summer-Comfort Sleeveless V-neck, page 104. Right: Daisy-Petals Ensemble, page 98.

Hug-Me, page 81

Simply Striped, page 49

Executive Editor: Rick Bailey
Editorial Director: Randy Summerlin
Editor: Judith Schuler
Art Director: Don Burton
Book Design: Leslie Sinclair
Typography: Cindy Coatsworth, Michelle Claridge
Designer/Consultant: Aline B. Sosne
Photography: Mike Zwerling
Cover Photo: Balfour Walker, Tucson, Arizona
Illustrations: Florence Temko and Doug Burton

HPBooks®
P.O. Box 5367
Tucson, Arizona 85703
(602) 888-2150
ISBN: 0-89586-268-9
Library of Congress Catalog Card Number: 83-82406
©1984 Florence Temko
Printed in U.S.A.

Here Comes the Gang, page 62.

Portuguese Fisherman's Knit, page 106.

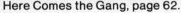

ABOUT THE AUTHOR

Florence Temko began knitting as a child and has enjoyed handcrafts all her life. The author of 20 previous how-to books is committed in this book to making knitting fun. Another goal is to present patterns that are simple, yet result in good-looking, well-fitting clothes.

In addition to writing books and articles, Mrs. Temko conducts hands-on workshops, classes and lectures in many places, including the Metropolitan Museum of Art in New York. She was educated in Great Britain at Wycombe Abbey School, London University and the New School for Social Research in New York City. She is listed in *Who's Who of American Women*. She lives with her husband in Lenox, in the Berkshire Hills of Massachusetts.

New Knitting is for You!

Hand knitting has recently become popular again. Beautiful, new yarns are being produced in lovely colors and textures. Designers are using these yarns to develop patterns that are quick and fun to knit. The shapes of sweaters are simpler to help fit knitting into your lifestyle.

This book will help you create many attractive garments and accessories. A collection of beautiful sweaters is divided into *New Classics,* beginning on page 48, and *New Dazzlers,* beginning on page 80. Sweaters include old favorites, such as crew-neck and V-neck sweaters. You'll also find new T-shirts and jackets. Some sweaters are block knits of simple rectangles. *Accessories and Small Things* are found on page 30.

Learning to Knit begins on page 5. Step-by-step instructions describe knitting methods and processes. It's helpful to beginning and expert knitters.

Sampler of Stitches, page 22, gives instructions for 19 different stitch patterns. Patterns are illustrated with photographs of knitted swatches. Whether you're looking for a bulky knit or light lace, you can find the right texture for your garment.

Designing Your Own, page 118, helps you produce garments to suit your own taste. You'll learn to mix sweater designs with different stitch patterns. The section provides helpful ideas on color combinations so you can create any garment you can imagine.

This book functions on four levels:
- As a learning primer.
- As a pattern manual for specific garments and accessories.
- As a guide for interchanging patterns and yarns.
- As a reference book.

Every effort has been made to ensure patterns, instructions and information are clear and accurate. Many knitters have tested instructions.

Let this book become a friend you can call to your side to answer questions and offer stimulating ideas. Enjoy the exciting, wonderful world of knitting!

Learning to Knit

This section introduces you to the basics needed to make *any* garment in this book. If you have never knitted, work three sample swatches as a learning project. Make one swatch in garter stitch, one in stockinette stitch and one in knit-one-purl-one ribbing. All stitch patterns are made with two basic, simple knitting stitches—*knit* and *purl.* You will be surprised how quickly knitting becomes a smooth, automatic process.

Directions for stitches and patterns are given as clearly as possible. Some people find it is easier to learn basics from another person rather than from printed instructions. Don't hesitate to ask a knitter to help you get started. Most knitters are happy to introduce someone to this creative pastime. Yarn shops often provide expert help and may offer knitting classes.

MEASUREMENTS

All pattern and garment measurements are given in inches and centimeters. Work in either measurement, but be consistent. If you start in inches, complete the project using inch measurements.

FOR LEFTIES

If you are left-handed, follow the instructions by reversing the words *left* and *right* in the directions. You may find it easier to pencil in these changes. It may also help to look at drawings reflected in a mirror.

ABOUT NEEDLES

Knitting needles are sold in pairs and numbered according to thickness. In yarn shops and other stores, you may find American and metric dimensions. Metric dimensions specify needle diameters in millimeters. The chart on page 6 lists equivalent sizes.

Different needle sizes are needed to work with yarns of various weights. Heavier needles are better for thick wool. Thinner needles are better for thin cotton yarn. Occasionally, needle thickness is used to influence the density of the knitted fabric. Working thin yarn on large needles produces a lacy texture.

All patterns specify needle size. Needle size is subject to change, depending on how tightly you knit. This is explained more fully in the section on *Gauge,* page 14.

Length—Ten-inch (25cm) needles are the most popular, but longer needles are available for working a lot of stitches in a row. See illustration below.

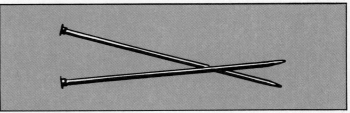

Pair of needles

Circular Needles—A circular needle has two pointed metal ends connected by metal or nylon wire. Circular needles are available in lengths ranging from 16 inches (40cm) to 36 inches (92cm). See illustration below.

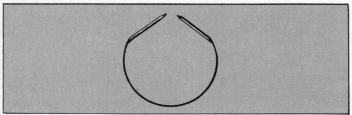
Circular needles

Circular needles are practical for two purposes—for knitting a seamless tube and as a substitute for straight needles when a large number of stitches is worked.

Tube knitting produces garments without side seams. With a pair of regular needles, knitting every row produces garter stitch. On a circular needle, knitting every row produces stockinette stitch. By *alternating* knit and purl rows on a circular needle, you create garter stitch.

To work tube knitting, cast on the required number of stitches in the usual way. Do not change the position of the needle. Continue working in the same direction. Work the *first* stitch you cast on as the first stitch of the new row. Keep working around the garment like a spiral. If you knit every stitch in every row, you produce stockinette stitch.

If you prefer seamless tube knitting, you can adjust a regular pattern for circular needles. Combine the number of stitches specified for the back and front. Cast on this total number of stitches and knit in a tube, as described above. When you reach the armholes, divide the tube into two flat parts for front and back. Change to straight needles and continue working according to the original pattern. A one-piece garment made with thick yarn on a circular needle is heavy near the end of the work.

Back-and-forth knitting can be done with circular needles when a large number of stitches is required in one row. Follow regular pattern instructions, and turn the work around at the end of each row. Knit back and forth from one end of the needle to the other.

Some knitters find the flexibility of circular needles comfortable. They choose circular needles most of the time and rarely use straight needles.

EQUIVALENCY CHART OF KNITTING NEEDLES

American Needles	Metric Needles in Millimeters
1	2-1/2
2	2-3/4
3	3-1/4
4	3-1/2
5	4
6	4-1/2
7	4-3/4
8	5
9	5-1/2
10	6
10-1/2	7
11	8

OTHER TOOLS

In addition to needles, you may need other knitting supplies.

Row-and-Stitch Counters—These are small cylindrical counters. Place one at the blunt end of a needle, and twirl it to show numbers. Numbers remind you where you are in the pattern, how many rows you have done or the number of stitches you've worked.

Ring Markers—Colored plastic or metal rings can be placed between stitches to serve as markers. They are slipped from the left needle to the right and carried from row to row. A paper clip or piece of yarn knotted in a circle can be used for the same purpose.

Cable Needles—These short needles are used to hold stitches temporarily when you knit cable patterns. Cable needles come in two sizes—regular and bulky. Double-pointed needles may be substituted for cable needles.

Stitch Holder—A stitch holder looks like an oversize safety pin. It is used to hold stitches until you are ready to work them again. You can also hold stitches on a piece of yarn knotted in a loop. Lift stitches off the knitting needle with a threaded embroidery needle, then tie yarn in a loop. You can also use large safety pins. See illustrations below.

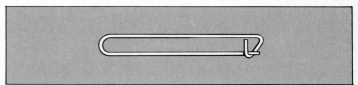
Stitch holder

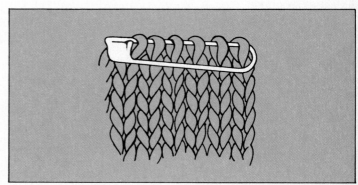
Stitches on a safety pin

Needle Measure—If you have unmarked needles, you can determine their size with a needle measure. A measure has holes the sizes of each needle diameter. Fit the needle neatly into one of the holes. The number next to the hole indicates the size of the needle.

Crochet Hooks—A crochet hook is useful for picking up dropped stitches and for seaming edges together. See page 17 for information on using a crochet hook to rescue dropped stitches. Almost any size crochet hook will do. You may find size G—international standard size 3.50—is a practical size.

ABOUT YARN

Knitting yarns range from thin, like sewing thread, to bulky, like rope. Yarns are technically divided into four basic types, ranging from fine to heavy. These basic types are *fingering, sport, worsted* and *bulky.* Sport-weight and worsted-weight yarn used to be called three-ply and four-ply yarns. Due to the increasing number of novelty yarns, distinctions are becoming blurred.

Dye Lots—Whatever yarn you choose, *always* buy enough to complete the work. Manufacturers dye large batches of yarn, but there are differences in color from one dye lot to another.

Some stores may take back extra yarn and give you a refund. Some specialty stores may give you a lower price if you agree *not* to return extra yarn. The store may not be able to sell the yarn because the dye lot may no longer be available.

Skeins, Balls or Hanks—Most yarns come in balls or skeins, ready to be worked. A few are packaged in *hanks,* a circle of yarn that must be wound into balls by the purchaser. Hang the circle of yarn over the back of a chair, and wind it from there. You can also have someone hold the loop of yarn over their outstretched wrists. Don't wind balls too tightly or you may stretch the yarn. Yarn winders are also available for this task.

Ply—Yarn is made of several strands twisted together. The number of strands varies from two to eight. A yarn consisting of two strands is called *2-ply,* and one made up of four strands is called *4-ply.* Occasionally a 4-ply yarn may be thinner than a 2-ply because the thickness of individual strands varies. Some yarns, such as *Icelandic,* are not twisted at all.

Composition of Yarn—Yarns can be natural, synthetic or a mixture of both fibers.

Natural yarns come from nature. For centuries, wool was the staple of knitting. Wool is warm, flexible and long-lasting. Other natural fibers are cotton, silk and linen. Rayon may also be considered natural because it's made from cellulose, the basic ingredient of vegetable matter.

In recent years, cotton has become a favorite for warm-weather wear. Manufacturers are creating interesting cotton yarns in many beautiful colors.

Synthetic yarns are man-made. The chemical industry produces synthetic yarns that imitate natural yarns. These yarns are easy to wash and often cost less than natural yarns. Orlon, made from acrylic, and nylon are the two most popular fibers. They are sold under many brand names.

Blends are combinations of natural and synthetic yarns. They take advantage of the desirable features of two or more fibers. A combination of acrylic, wool and mohair gives you the advantages of the easy care and low cost of acrylic, the natural absorbency and flexibility of wool and the luxurious feel and light weight of mohair.

Luxury yarns, such as mohair, cashmere, silk, angora and alpaca, are frequently mixed with other fibers. They add softness and fluffiness to the yarn. Linen is strong and cool to wear. Because of its high cost, it's usually combined with other yarns.

Substituting Yarn—At the beginning of each knitting pattern, you will find information about the type of yarns suitable for making a garment. This is followed by a description of the yarn actually used in the sweater shown in the photograph. You may want to select a different yarn. If you do, it must knit up to the same gauge as specified in the pattern.

To help select your yarn, you may want to look at a printed yarn-interchange chart at a knitting store. This groups together yarns that knit up to the same gauge. If you don't want to buy a chart, you may be able to borrow one.

When substituting yarns, purchase enough to complete your garment or project. Yarns from different manufacturers are produced in different weights and lengths. If you need a certain number of balls in one brand, you may need a different amount in another brand.

Your choice of yarns is large. Whatever yarn you choose, you must work to the gauge specified for the *pattern.* If you don't, the size of the garment or project will not be correct, and it might not fit.

Given the choice, select yarns of the best quality in your price range. When the garment is complete, you'll enjoy the beauty of your work for a long time.

Leftover Yarn—Any yarns you have left can be used to make a hat or other small accessory. They can also be used for stripes, patches or color accents in another garment. Throughout the book you will find suggestions to help use yarn left from other knitting projects.

ABOUT PATTERNS

When you first look at the patterns in this book, you may find the presentation unusual. Numbers for stitches, rows, inches, centimeters and other indicators are separated from the text. See example below.

Numbers for a particular size are listed in a *vertical* column. When you're ready to knit, draw a line with a marker around the numbers or highlight the entire column for the size you plan to make. Your eyes will concentrate on the appropriate figures. If you want to repeat the same pattern in a different size, circle or highlight that column with a marker in a different color.

Work even for total length of	12 (30	14 36	16 40	19-1/2 50	20-1/2 52	21-1/2 55	23 59	25 64	27 inches 69cm)
This is 1-1/2 inches (4cm) less than desired length to shoulder. Work knit-2-purl-2 ribbing for	1-1/2 (4	1-1/2 4	1-1/2 4	1-1/2 4	1-1/2 4	1-1/2 4	1-1/2 4	1-1/2 4	1-1/2 inches 4cm)
Bind off loosely in pattern.									

Numbers for each size are listed in a vertical column. Circle or highlight the column of the size you want to knit, as shown above.

Instructions are given in inches and centimeters. Before you start, cross out the system you will *not* use. There will be less confusion when reading directions.

Mark the pattern with other notes, such as type of yarn used or alterations made. This will help you the next time you knit the garment or project. The arrangement of pattern instructions makes it easy to follow a pattern in the size you select.

Most patterns include a section called *Design Your Own*. This section offers ideas on ways to change and adapt basic patterns to suit your personal desires.

SIZES

Size is important when you buy clothes. If you're a knitter, the right size is always in stock. Pattern directions in this book are often given for small, medium and large sizes. These sizes are the most satisfactory for contemporary clothing. Sizes are based on actual chest measurements, with the finished garment about 2 inches (5cm) larger. This allows for a comfortable fit. For loose-fitting sweaters, built-in allowances may be even greater. Consult the size chart, page 21, to help you select the correct size.

How to Measure Yourself—Hold the measuring tape comfortably across the widest part of the chest. If possible, let another person take the measurement. For women's garments, bra size is usually a good guide for body chest measurements.

How to Measure Knitting—Measure the knitted garment

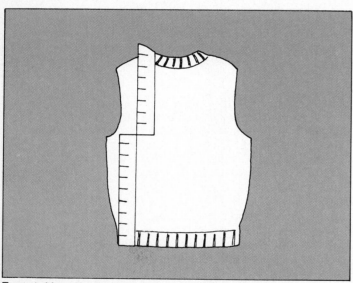

For total length, measure from waist to underarm and add measurement from underarm to shoulder.

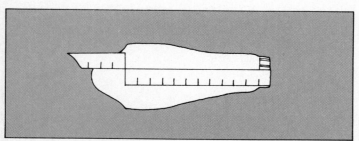

Measure cap of sleeve. Measure length of sleeve to underarm.

in straight lines, not around curves. See illustrations below.

If You're Not an Average Size—We're all individuals and built differently, but ready-made clothing comes in standard sizes. You know where you need alterations, such as shortening sleeves or lengthening the waist. When you knit a garment, you can suit your personal requirements. In *Designing Your Own*, beginning on page 118, you will find specific directions for personal fit.

TERMS AND ABBREVIATIONS

If you're new to knitting, you may have seen knitting patterns and thought they were hieroglyphics: *K2, yn fwd, *sl 2, yn back* K2.*

In this book, basic English is used in patterns. When you understand the information in this *Learning to Knit* section, you should be able to follow pattern instructions. Two terms need some further explanation.

Asterisks (*)—These are important symbols. When you see them in a pattern, it means *repeat the pattern from the asterisk*. Keep repeating the pattern according to exact instructions.

In a pattern you might find: **Knit 4, purl 2; repeat from * across row.* This means you repeat knit 4, purl 2 until you reach the end of the row.

In another example, you might find: **Knit 3, purl 3; repeat from * across, end row with knit 2.* This means the repeating pattern of knit 3, purl 3 does not divide exactly into the number of stitches you have on the needle. You will end up with 2 knit stitches.

Abbreviations—The following list may help you understand abbreviations used in other patterns.

beg	beginning
dec	decrease
g st	garter stitch
inc	increase
psso	pass slipped stitch over
rem	remaining
rep	repeat
sl	slip
st st	stockinette stitch
tog	together
yon	yarn over needle

KNITTING BEGINS

Enough of preliminaries! It's time to get out the needles and yarn, and start working. It may help to read instructions one line at a time *out loud* to yourself as you proceed with each step.

CASTING ON

Beginning the first row of stitches is called *casting on*. It's achieved by making a chain of loops next to each other on a knitting needle. There are directions for two methods. For the first method, *one needle* is required. For the second method, which is similar to regular knitting, *two needles* are used.

With either method, you can cast on with needles that are one or two sizes larger than those specified for the pattern. This is helpful if you have a tendency to cast on tightly. Change to the specified size for the first row of ribbing or knitting after casting on.

One-Needle Method—As you read these instructions, refer to illustrations below. They may help clarify the procedure for you.

Make a slip knot about 36 inches from the end of the yarn. This distance will vary, depending on how many stitches must be cast on. Allow about 1 inch (2-1/2cm) for each stitch. Place the loop on the needle, and tighten it until it slides comfortably along the needle.

Hold the needle in your right hand like a pencil. Place the yarn leading to the ball over your thumb. Place the loose end of the yarn over your left index finger. Grasp both yarns with the other three fingers of the left hand.

Bring the needle down in front of your left thumb, forming a loop on the thumb. Insert the needle under and up into this loop. Next, move the needle under the yarn coming from your left index finger. Draw the yarn through the loop from your thumb, and slip the loop off. Gently pull yarn away from the needle to tighten the stitch.

Repeat making loops on the needle until the required number of stitches are cast on. Push stitches along the needle toward the knobbed end as you work.

One-Needle Method of Casting On

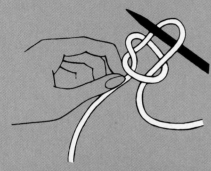

1. Make a slip knot, and place loop on needle.

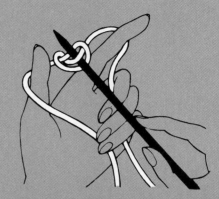

2. Hold needle in your right hand, and form a loop over your thumb.

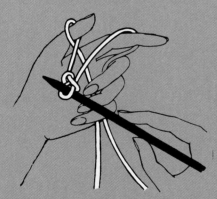

3. Tighten loop on right needle.

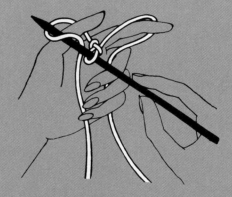

4. Insert needle under and up into loop.

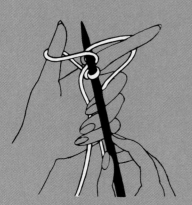

5. Move needle across and under yarn on index fingers.

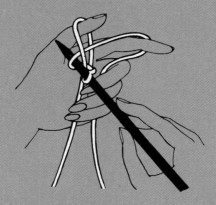

6. Draw yarn through loop from thumb.

Knitting-On Method—As you read these instructions, refer to illustrations below. They may help clarify the procedure for you.

Make a slip knot and place the loop on the needle. Tighten it until it slides comfortably along the needle. This is your first stitch.

Hold the needle with the loop of yarn in your left hand. From the front, near you, insert the right needle under the left needle. Loop the yarn coming from the ball over your right index finger. Let the yarn drop behind. Grasp the yarn inside your palm with your other three fingers. See illustration 1 below for proper positioning of hands.

With the right index finger, loop the yarn over the point of the right needle, from the bottom up. Draw the yarn through the loop toward you. Place the new loop on the left needle by digging in, or inserting, the left needle from right to left. Withdraw the right needle.

Repeat this process until you cast on the required number of stitches on the left needle. Push stitches along the needle toward the knobbed end as you work.

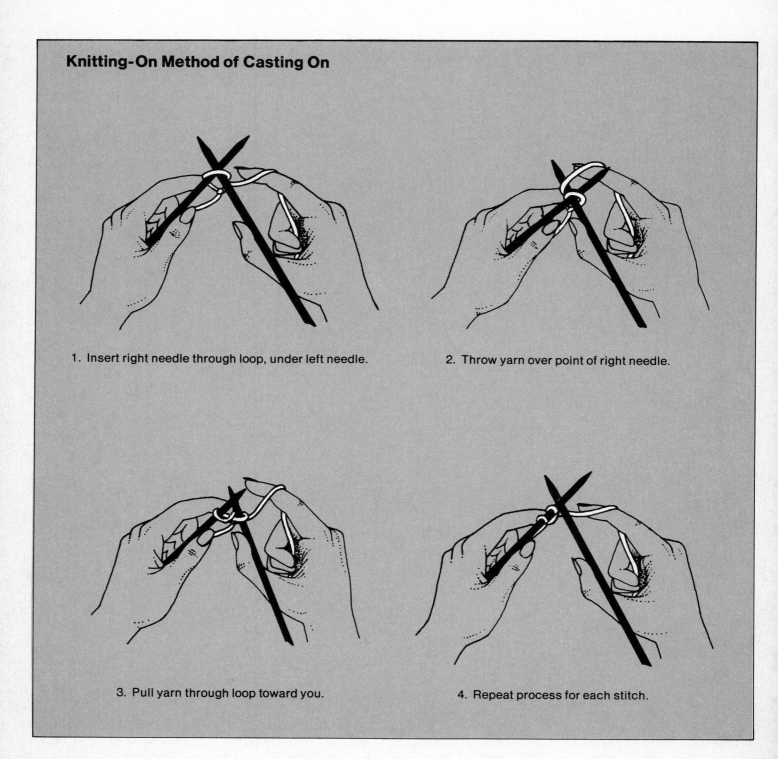

Knitting-On Method of Casting On

1. Insert right needle through loop, under left needle.

2. Throw yarn over point of right needle.

3. Pull yarn through loop toward you.

4. Repeat process for each stitch.

KNIT STITCH

After you have cast on, you're ready to work the first row in the *knit stitch*. As you read these instructions, refer to illustrations below. They may help clarify the procedure for you.

Hold the needle with the stitches you cast on in your *left* hand. Your left index finger holds the first stitch lightly. With the right hand, hold the empty needle as you would a pencil.

Place the yarn coming from the ball over your right index finger. Let the yarn drop behind. Grasp the yarn inside your palm with your other three fingers. See the first illustration below for proper positioning of hands.

Insert the right needle into the front of the first stitch on the left needle. The point of the right needle passes under the left needle and rests on your left forefinger.

With your right index finger, loop the yarn under and over the point of the right needle. Draw the yarn through the stitch on the left needle with the point of the right needle. Slip the stitch off the left needle. Your first knit stitch is now on the right needle.

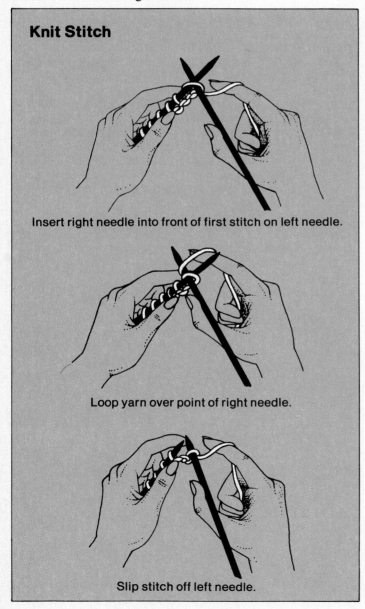

Knit Stitch

Insert right needle into front of first stitch on left needle.

Loop yarn over point of right needle.

Slip stitch off left needle.

Repeat this process until all the stitches are knitted off the left needle. Move stitches along the left needle as you work. The stitch being knitted is always close to the point of the needle.

BEGINNING A NEW ROW

Switch the needle with the stitches you have just knitted from your right to your left hand. The empty needle is held in your *right* hand. Begin working the same way as you did the first row.

GARTER STITCH

When you knit row after row, you create a pattern called *garter stitch*. See illustration below.

Garter stitch is created with rows of knit stitches.

PURL STITCH

As you read these instructions, refer to illustrations on page 12. They may help clarify the procedure for you.

To make a purl stitch, insert the needle from the right to the left in the front of the stitch. This is the *opposite* direction than the knit stitch. The yarn drops in front, which is the side toward you.

Hold needles the same way you hold them for working knit stitches. The needle with the stitches is in your *left* hand. Your left index finger holds the first stitch lightly. With the right hand, hold the empty needle as you would a pencil.

Place the yarn from the ball over your right index finger. Grasp the yarn inside your palm with your other three fingers.

Insert the empty needle into the first stitch from right to left, in the front of the left needle. Loop yarn behind the right needle, then under its point.

With the point of the right needle, draw the yarn through the stitch. Slip the stitch off the left needle. Your first purl stitch is now on the right needle.

Repeat this process until all stitches are purled off the left needle. Push stitches along the needle toward the knobbed end as you work.

Purl Stitch

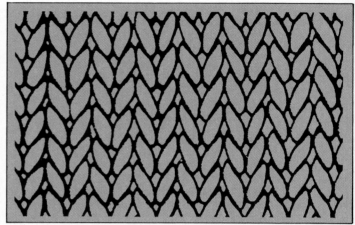

Insert right needle from right to left into front of stitch.

Loop yarn behind, then under, point of right needle.

Slip stitch off left needle.

STOCKINETTE STITCH

Alternating rows of knit stitches with rows of purl stitches creates a pattern called *stockinette stitch*. See illustration below.

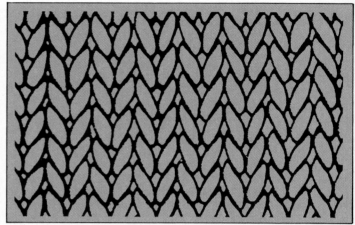

Stockinette stitch is created by alternating rows of knit stitches and purl stitches.

KNIT-ONE-PURL-ONE RIBBING

Knit and purl stitches can be alternated *within a row* to produce many patterns. Vertical ribbing is made when a knit stitch and purl stitch alternate across the row. See illustration below. An *even number* of stitches must be cast on at the beginning.

Follow this procedure: Knit the first stitch. Before you make the purl stitch, swing the yarn between the tips of the needles to the front. Make a regular purl stitch.

The next stitch is a knit stitch. Swing the yarn from the front to the back, then make your knit stitch. Repeat these two stitches across the row.

This ribbing pattern is knit one, purl one.

WORK EVEN

You may see the instruction *work even for x inches (xcm)*. Continue working in the appropriate pattern on the existing number of stitches without increasing or decreasing stitches. Work until you reach the specified measurement.

SLIP ONE

When you are instructed to *slip one,* slip a stitch from the left to the right needle *without* working the stitch.

Insert the right needle as if to knit or purl, depending on the pattern. Slip the stitch onto the right needle without working it. Work the *next* stitch as indicated in the pattern.

YARN OVER

When you read the instruction *yarn over,* wind the yarn over the tip of the right needle from front to back. Knit the next stitch the regular way.

BINDING OFF

Binding off means you have reached a milestone in your work. If you bind off all the stitches, you have completed a piece of the garment or project. If you bind off only a few stitches, you have usually reached the armhole or neckline.

Follow this procedure: Knit or purl the first two stitches, according to the pattern. With the left needle, pass the first stitch over the second stitch and off the tip of the right needle. See illustrations below. This leaves one stitch on the right needle. Knit the next stitch and repeat the process. Continue until all stitches except one are bound off.

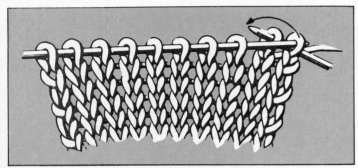

Work first two stitches. Pass first stitch over second stitch and over tip of right needle.

Three stitches bound off.

Cut the yarn a few inches from the edge of the knitting. Draw the end of the yarn through the last stitch, and pull out the needle. Leave the end of the yarn hanging down.

Pattern instructions often state: *Bind off loosely.* This is to remind you to avoid binding off more tightly than your gauge. This can cause distortion in the garment and may lead to problems, such as necklines that don't fit comfortably over the head.

Instructions may also state: *Bind off in pattern.* This means you bind off in the pattern you are working. If you are binding off while working in ribbing, work knit and purl stitches across the row, as required. Then bind off.

SHAPING

Some patterns in this book are knitted in blocks, straight up and down. Many garments are shaped by increasing and decreasing. Shaping can be achieved in several ways.

Increasing One Stitch—Knitting twice into one stitch is the most commonly used method. You knit into the front of the stitch, then into the back of the same stitch.

Follow this procedure: Knit or purl a stitch the regular way. Do not let it drop off the left needle. Slide the right needle behind, and make a new stitch through the back of the loop. Slip the old stitch off the needle. Continue working the garment. See illustrations below.

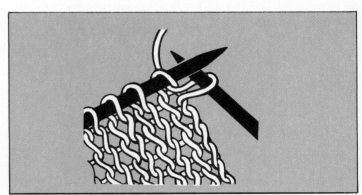

Work regular stitch. Slide right needle behind, and make new stitch through back of loop.

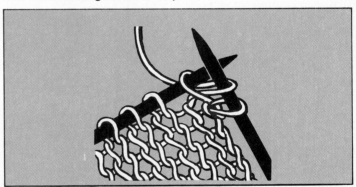

Slip both stitches off needle.

Catch an In-Between Stitch—You can also make an extra stitch by picking up the connecting yarn between two stitches and knitting it. With the right needle, lift the yarn between two stitches, and place it on the left needle. Knit or purl this loop.

Row-Below Pick-Up—This is another method for making an extra stitch. Before you knit or purl the next stitch in the row, knit or purl in the stitch *below* it. Knit or purl the next stitch the regular way.

Increasing at the Edge—If the pattern calls for increasing one stitch at the beginning or end of a row, work the edge stitch regularly. Form the increase on the *second* stitch.

Increasing Several Stitches—You may have to add several stitches at the beginning or end of a row. Cast on the required number of stitches with the knitting-on method of casting on, as described on page 9.

Increasing Evenly Across Row—A pattern may call for increasing a number of stitches evenly across a row. This occurs frequently between ribbing and the main body of a sweater.

Divide the number of stitches on the needle by the number to be added. The result will be the number of stitches *between* each interval. If you have 88 stitches and are asked to increase 8 stitches, 88 divided by 8 equals 11. Increase one stitch every 11th stitch across the row.

Decreasing One Stitch—Knit or purl two stitches together as though they are one. For *knitting* two stitches together, insert the right needle from the left through the back of the first stitch, through the second. Work the loops together as one. See illustration below.

For *purling* two stitches together, insert the right needle from right to left in front, through two stitches. Work the two loops together as one.

Work two stitches together.

Slip off needle.

Binding Off Several Stitches—You can bind off several stitches at the beginning of a row or in the middle of a row. Follow regular binding-off instructions. Work the remaining stitches the usual way.

KNIT THREE LEARNING SWATCHES

Making three swatches in three different stitch patterns is a good way to learn to knit. You can use worsted-weight yarn and size-8 needles, but other supplies will do as well.

Garter Stitch—Knitting every stitch in every row is called *garter stitch*. For your learning swatch, cast on 30 stitches. Knit each row until the piece measures 4 inches (10cm) in length.

You may need some help casting on or making a knit stitch. See the previous discussions for the following techniques: casting on, page 8; knit stitch, page 11; beginning a new row, page 11; and binding off, page 13.

Stockinette Stitch—The stitch pattern produced by alternating rows of knit and purl stitches is called *stockinette stitch*. For your swatch, cast on 30 stitches.

You may need some help casting on, knitting or purling. See the previous discussions for the following techniques: casting on, page 8; knit stitch, page 11; beginning a new row, page 11; purl stitch, page 11 and binding off, page 13. Alternate knit rows and purl rows until the piece measures 4 inches (10cm). Bind off.

Knit-One-Purl-One Ribbing—Cast on 30 stitches. On the first row, knit a stitch, then purl a stitch. Continue alternating knit and purl stitches to the end of the row. Repeat this process until the piece measures 4 inches (10cm). Bind off.

PREFERRED KNITTING METHODS

Illustrations of knitting methods show yarn being held with the right hand. Some knitters feed yarn from the left hand. This is a matter of personal preference. Both methods produce identical results.

Some people prefer to knit one way rather than another. Preference usually depends on who taught them. Different methods seem to originate from different European countries. In any case, whatever feels right to you is right.

THE GAUGE

Your success depends on working to the correct gauge. *Gauge* is the number of stitches and rows per inch in hand knitting. You must match your gauge with the pattern's required gauge. If you don't, you may be disappointed with the garment or project. After spending hours working on a garment, you may find it's too tight or it's big enough for two people.

Knit a sample swatch before you begin *every* garment. Work a 4-inch (10cm) square in the chosen stitch pattern with the selected yarn and needles. Measure the number of stitches horizontally and the number of rows vertically. If they do not conform *exactly* to the gauge specified for your pattern, make another swatch.

A small inaccuracy on a sample is multiplied in a finished garment. Keep making swatches until you have the correct gauge.

You may ask why a pattern calls for a particular-size needle. A designer specifies the needle size for a fictitious average person. Use the specified needle size as a starting point for your test swatch. If you need *more* stitches to the inch, work another swatch in needles one size *smaller*. If you need *fewer* stitches to the inch, work in needles one size *larger*.

Knitters work at a tension that is comfortable for them. Don't try to knit more tightly or loosely to achieve the correct gauge. Sooner or later you will revert to the natural tension of your knitting.

Make a Gauge Swatch—It's important to make a gauge swatch before you begin any new project. Look at the gauge specified in your pattern. Let's say the gauge specified is:

5 stitches = 1 inch (2-1/2cm)
6 rows = 1 inch (2-1/2cm) approximately

To produce a 4-inch (10cm) swatch, multiply the stitch number specified per inch by the number of inches you want to knit. For this example, it is 5 x 4 = 20. You would cast on 20 stitches. Use needles in the size specified for the

stitch pattern. Work the stitch pattern over 20 stitches until the piece measures 4 inches (10cm). Bind off.
Measure Gauge Swatch—Place the swatch on a hard surface, and lightly pat it flat with your hand. Put the edge of a metal or wood ruler on top of the swatch, near the center. See photos below.

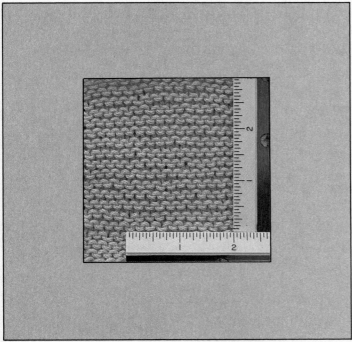

The gauge on this swatch, worked in garter stitch, is:
5 stitches = 1 inch (2-1/2cm)
10 rows (or 5 ridges) = 1 inch (2-1/2cm)

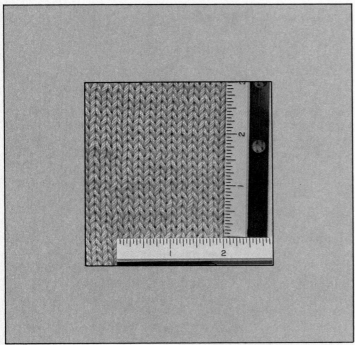

The gauge on this swatch, worked in stockinette stitch, is:
5 stitches = 1 inch (2-1/2cm)
7 rows = 1 inch (2-1/2cm)

For the horizontal count, which is the number of stitches, count the number of stitches that make up 1 inch (2-1/2cm). For our example, if you count 5 stitches, you are on target. If you have only 4-1/2 stitches, make another swatch with needles one size *smaller*. If you have 5-1/2 stitches, make another swatch with needles one size *larger*.

For the vertical count, which is the number of rows, measure the number of rows that make up 1 inch (2-1/2cm). For our example, if you count six rows, you are on target. If you have only five rows per inch (2-1/2cm), using needles a size *smaller* brings you closer to gauge. If you count seven rows, you should use needles a size *larger*.
Matching Horizontal and Vertical Count—Horizontal and vertical adjustments usually complement each other. But the *horizontal stitch count* is more important. It's easier to adjust length than the width. The number of rows add up to the length of the garment, which is usually specified as a measurement, not a number of rows. If you have to choose, adjust your gauge to the horizontal stitch count. *Knit a sample swatch every time!*

KEEP CHECKING

Your gauge may change as you proceed with your work. Usually the tension becomes a little looser as you become more familiar with the pattern. The weight of the fabric may become heavier as you go along. Or you may be a knitter whose work tightens up. Keep checking your gauge as you work on your project.
Don't Swap Knitting with Someone Else—Two people may knit exactly the same gauge, yet produce a slightly different texture. Keep this in mind if you are thinking of asking someone to work on your project. In rough textures, variations are less noticeable.

JOINING BALLS OF YARN

When you finish one ball of yarn, you have to join a new one. Make the joining as inconspicuous as possible. Try to start a new skein at the beginning of a row. Knot the two yarns together close to the edge of the row. Cut off both ends, leaving a 6-inch (15cm) tail. Before you put the garment together, release the knot. Thread each yarn tail through a broad-eye needle. Weave the ends into the backs of the stitches or up and down the edge.

If you are short of yarn and must economize, join yarns in the middle of a row. When weaving the ends of yarn into the garment, be sure ends don't go through to the front. With thick yarn, cut away half the thickness to reduce bulk. Leave 1/2 inch (1cm) of full thickness near the joining.

STRIPES AND OTHER COLOR CHANGES

If you want to use more than one color, do it with stripes. Stripes can be worked in stockinette stitch or another stitch pattern.
Horizontal Stripes—To make horizontal stripes, change colors at the beginning of a new row. Knot the old and new yarns together the same way you join balls of yarn. Repeat this procedure each time you begin another color. When the garment is finished, weave the ends of the yarn into backs of stitches of the same color. In stockinette stitch, always begin a new color at the beginning of a knit row.

Narrow Stripes—If stripes are less than 3/4 inch (2cm) wide, and only in two colors, don't break yarn when you change color. On the first color change, knot the new yarn at the beginning of the row. You will have two balls of yarn attached. Work the second color stripe in the normal way. When you are ready to use the first color again, guide the yarn up the side. Before making the first stitch with the new color, twist yarns around each other. Allow enough slack on the yarn carried up so the edge of the work doesn't pucker. Work the row the usual way. Repeat this procedure each time you change colors.

Vertical Stripes—True vertical striping is done by twisting together yarns of different colors in the middle of a row. This type of striping is more complicated than horizontal stripes.

It is possible to make simple vertical stripes by working a sweater sideways. You begin knitting the back and front of a sweater at the side instead of the bottom. Change colors the same way as for horizontal stripes. The *Child's Jacket,* page 57, is worked with this method.

Practice Swatch—Practice vertical color changes by making a two-color sample swatch. Cast on 20 stitches and knit stockinette stitch. Change color after 10 stitches. Twist yarns around each other to avoid a small hole. Continue working and repeating the color change on every row until you are comfortable with this method.

SEWING TOGETHER

There are four recommended methods for joining parts of garments together. These methods are *back-stitch, over-stitch, weaving together* and *knitting together.* You may prefer one method over another for different situations. Specific advantages for each are discussed below.

For the two sewing methods, place the two pieces to be joined on top of each other, with right-sides together. Pin them together with regular straight pins so both ends are even. Knit garments can be stretched a bit to fit, so fitting pieces together should not be a problem.

Back-Stitch—Thread a blunt, broad-eye needle with yarn left from casting on, or use a separate piece of yarn. Insert the needle into the work, and make a full stitch. To make the next stitch, insert the needle a half-stitch back. Take another full stitch. Repeat this process until the seam is sewn. See illustration below.

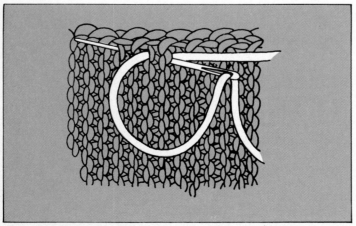

Stitch pieces together by inserting needle into both knit pieces and making full back-stitch.

Over-Stitch—To over-stitch both edges, insert the needle from the front to the back of each stitch. Make one over-stitch for each knit stitch. Work at a tension that keeps the seam flat, but leaves no gap between pieces. At the end of the seam, back-stitch a couple of inches, then cut yarn.

Weaving Together—Weaving seams together gives a smooth look to flat knitting, such as stockinette stitch. Place edges of the two pieces to be seamed side by side, with right-sides up and ends even.

Place a strip of narrow masking tape across the seam every few inches to keep the seam in position. Thread a blunt, broad-eye needle with yarn left from casting on, or use a separate piece of yarn.

On the right-side of the seam, slip the needle between the edge stitch and next stitch. Carry the sewing needle and yarn over to the left side. Pick up the yarn between the first two stitches on that side. Slip the needle through the edge stitch, and pull the sewing yarn snug. Go to the right side again. Continue alternating sides along the seam. See illustration below.

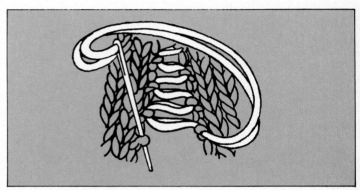

Pick up edge stitches from each piece.

Pull the sewing yarn tight enough so edge stitches disappear into the seam. The two pieces now butt together invisibly. At the end of the seam, back-stitch a couple of inches, then cut yarn.

Knitting Seams Together—This method produces invisible seams when two pieces are worked together. Knitting seams together is attractive for shoulder seams, but use this method whenever possible.

Do not bind off shoulder stitches on the garment back and fronts. Transfer stitches to stitch holders or extra knitting needles.

When you're ready to knit seams together, put stitches for each section on a separate knitting needle. Place back and front shoulder sections together with *right-sides facing.* Both needle points face right. Attach yarn from the skein at the edge of your work. With a third needle, knit together one stitch from the front and one from the back. See illustration on page 17.

Knit the next two stitches together the same way. When you have two stitches on the third needle, bind off one stitch. Pull the first stitch over the second stitch. Continue along the shoulder until all stitches are bound off. When you are finished, weave the end of the yarn invisibly in the wrong-side of the work.

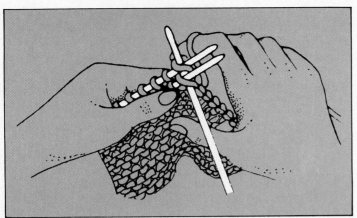

With third needle, knit together one stitch from the front and one from the back. After knitting two stitches, begin binding off.

WHERE DID YOU LEAVE OFF?

You can't always finish your work from beginning to end without interruption. When you are ready to pick up again, you must find out where you stopped in the pattern.

Knit or Purl?—When checking your work, it's not hard to tell the difference between the two basic stitches. *Knit* stitches look like V's. *Purl* stitches look like horizontal bars. See illustrations below.

Knit

Purl

Planned Interruption—Try to complete a row before stopping. If necessary, make a note to yourself where you left off. You can also purchase a small counter to attach to the blunt end of a needle. It is twirled to indicate the number of pattern rows completed.

Sudden Interruption—When interrupted suddenly, you may jump up and drop your work, even in the middle of a row. When you are ready to continue, you must figure out what comes next.

In some cases, what to do next is obvious. With garter stitch, continue with knit stitches. With stockinette stitch, check to see if you are working on a knit or purl row.

Determining Last Stitch Made—The yarn *always* hangs from the side you have already worked. If the yarn hangs *behind* the work, away from you, you *knitted* the last stitch. If the yarn hangs *in front,* on the side facing you, you *purled* the last stitch.

With more complicated patterns, compare the number of knit and purl stitches in the pattern with the number of stitches on the right needle. Match the number of stitches to the pattern. If necessary, count the number of rows.

FIXING MISTAKES

To err is human, and even the best knitters make a mistake once in awhile. Here are some common remedies.

Dropped Stitches—If you drop a stitch and it disappears three rows down, you can fix it. Use a crochet hook or the tip of the knitting needle. See illustrations below.

Knit-stitch rescue

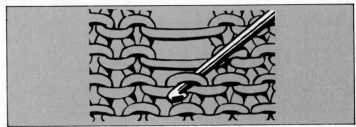

Purl-stitch rescue

To rescue a knit stitch, look closely at your work. You will see the dropped stitch as a loop with three horizontal strands above it. Insert a crochet hook in the loop. Pull the first ring of the ladder *over* it. This lifts the stitch up one row. Repeat this procedure until you have restored the stitch to the current row.

To rescue a purl stitch, look closely at your work. Do the same thing as for the knit-stitch rescue. With a purl stitch, keep the strand of yarn in *front* of the stitch to be lifted.

Many people find rescuing knit stitches is easier. You can convert a purl-stitch rescue into a knit-stitch rescue by turning the work to the other side.

Mixed-Pattern Rescue—Determine whether your work requires a knit or purl stitch to be rescued. Work from the front for a knit stitch and from the back for a purl stitch.

Undoing Several Rows—You may make a mistake in the pattern and not realize it until several rows have been worked. You will have to undo the rows that are affected.

Slip the work off the needle. Slowly pull yarn to unravel the rows. Do this until you reach the row of the last correct pattern. Using one of the empty needles, pick up all the stitches in the row. The last stitch in the row to be picked up is at the edge where the yarn hangs down. Count to be sure you have the correct number of stitches on the needle before continuing your regular pattern. If you find some twisted stitches as you work the next row, turn them around before working them.

Undoing Several Stitches—You may discover an error in the row you are working on or the row just below it. Sometimes it's better to undo the rows one stitch at a time.

Slip the left needle into the stitch *under* the last stitch on the right needle. Drop the stitch off the right needle, and pull the yarn out of the loop. Repeat this procedure until you reach the error. See illustrations below.

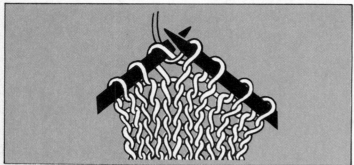
Slip left needle into last stitch on right needle.

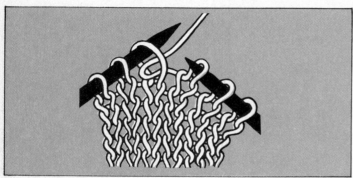
Drop stitch off right needle and pull yarn.

Check it Over — When you complete any rescue, examine the work for correctness, and rework it if necessary. A repaired stitch may be coarser, but stretching the knit fabric by gently pulling it may even out roughness. Pressing may also help.

WASHING AND DRY-CLEANING

Follow manufacturers' recommendations for yarn care. Many people have knitted garments dry-cleaned. Knitted cotton garments made of more than one color must be dry-cleaned because dyes may bleed. Tell the dry-cleaner about the yarn so extra care can be given, if necessary.

Usually manufacturers guarantee washability if yarn is composed of at least 70% synthetics. Often knitted garments are hand-washed, with the exception of cottons with mixed colors. Always use cool water — this is essential with wool. Warm water shrinks and mats wool fibers together. Some garments with a firm texture can be machine-washed in cool water on the delicate setting.

For hand-washing, fill the sink or pan with cool water. Add special detergent made for wool or use mild, non-detergent soap. You may use liquid-dishwashing detergent.

Use a few drops of detergent and some water on any spots you find. Do this for the cuffs and neckline if they are soiled. Gently squeeze these areas a few times to dislodge dirt. Be careful not to destroy the fuzz. Any lather you create will penetrate the fabric.

Immerse the garment in the suds. Let it soak for a few minutes. Squeeze the garment several times, swishing it around in the water. Do not pull or rub it.

Lift the garment out of the water. Gently squeeze out as much water as possible, then discard the suds. Rinse the garment by gently squeezing it in clean, lukewarm water. Rinse it in at least two changes of water until all traces of suds are gone.

Place the garment on a towel, and roll garment and towel up together. Pat or press the towel to remove moisture from the garment. Unroll it and spread the garment on a clean, dry towel placed on a hard, flat surface, such as a countertop. Shape the garment to the correct size, and let it dry for about 24 hours. Cotton knitteds may take two or three days to dry, depending on weather conditions.

BLOCKING

Blocking is the process of shaping knitted garments or projects. Garments are moistened, then pinned in the desired shape. They are left to dry naturally or pressed with an iron. Most garments do not need blocking. It is necessary to block a garment if it is lopsided or needs to be stretched. Blocking can increase a garment's size by as much as one full size.

Blocking takes advantage of the elasticity of knitted fabrics. If yarns are pushed into a desired shape while damp, they remain that way when dry. This is true of wools and, to a lesser extent, synthetics and cottons.

How to Block — Measure across the chest of a garment. Push or pull the garment into the proper size and shape. Lightly dampen the garment, then pin it to a large towel or rug. Stick straight pins into the garment at an angle. Be sure pins are the non-rusting type.

For a more professional job, lay the unblocked sweater flat on a piece of brown paper. Trace around it with pencil, then draw new lines for the desired shape. See illustration below. Place the paper on top of a large towel or rug. Dampen the garment lightly, and pin it to fit the new pattern. Let the garment dry or steam with an iron.

Professional blocking by a dry-cleaner or knitting store is recommended for coats, heavy garments, highly textured knitting and problem situations.

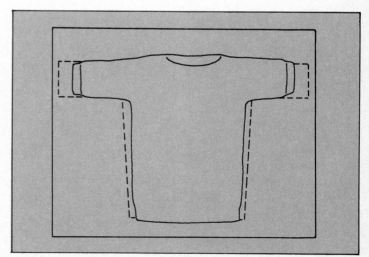
To block, lay garment on paper, and draw new lines for desired shape.

Steaming—If an inappropriate bulge appears on a garment, press it out. Smooth out the garment on top of a thick towel. Press the garment by placing a slightly damp cloth on top of it. Adjust the setting on the iron for the composition of the yarn. Don't allow the full weight of the iron to rest on the cloth or garment. Steam fluffy and hairy yarns from the wrong-side so you don't flatten them.

BUTTONHOLES

Some garments and projects need buttonholes. Always knit the side with the buttons first—left front for women, right front for men. Then it's easy to know where to place buttonholes!

Buttonhole Placement—Place the rim of one button 1/2 inch (1cm) above the bottom edge. Place the rim of another button close to the neck edge. Evenly divide the length between these two buttons for additional buttons.

It may help to make a pattern. Cut a paper strip the length of the border. Mark the positions of the buttons with horizontal lines. For five buttons, divide the strip into six spaces. For six buttons, divide the strip into seven spaces. See illustration below.

On the other front band, make knit-in buttonholes opposite the place where buttons are located. When a neckband is knitted separately, the top buttonhole is 1/2 inch (1cm) below the final neck edge.

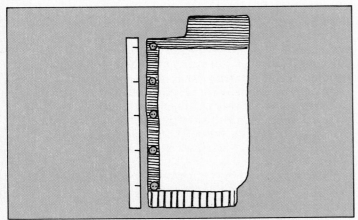

When placing buttonholes, cut a paper strip the length of the border. Mark it with position of buttonholes, and match marks to pattern.

Small, Round Buttonholes—For a small button, make an eyelet hole. When you reach the place for the buttonhole, loop the yarn over the needle. Knit or purl the next two stitches together. In the next row, continue in your regular pattern. See illustration below.

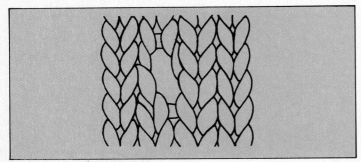

Small, round buttonholes

Horizontal Buttonholes—Horizontal buttonholes on cardigans and jackets are placed in the middle of the band, directly down from the center of the neck. Measure the button, and calculate the nearest even number of stitches that make this size. If you have a 3/4-inch (2cm) button and are working a gauge of four stitches to the inch, the buttonhole is three stitches wide.

When you reach the place for the buttonhole, bind off the required number of stitches. In the next row, when you reach the buttonhole, cast stitches on again. Turn the work around to cast on. After casting on, turn your work around again and continue working the row. See illustrations below.

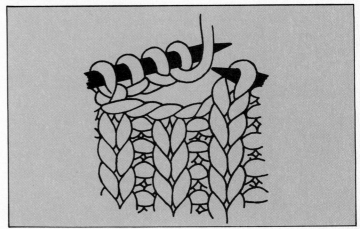

Buttonhole in progress.

Completed buttonhole.

Over-stitching buttonholes

Over-Stitching—To keep their shape, sew around finished buttonholes with a buttonhole-stitch. See illustration on page 19.

ADD-ONS

Pockets, patches and tassels add a special touch to any garment. Make them in contrasting colors as bright accents to almost any garment.

Pockets and Patches—Pockets and patches can add a distinctive look to a garment. They can be worked in rectangles, circles and other shapes.

First make the pockets or patches in the desired shape, then determine the correct place for them on the garment. Sew patches to the garment around all edges, but leave the upper edges of pockets open. If knitted to the same gauge as the main fabric, align stitches and rows on both pieces exactly.

Sew pockets and patches to the garment with the following method. Thread a broad-eye needle with a length of yarn, then pick up a stitch from the garment. Pick up a stitch from the pocket. Pick up another stitch from the main fabric. Keep alternating stitching this way.

Tassels—Tassels are great to add to children's and adults' clothing. As you read instructions, refer to illustrations below. They may help clarify the procedure for you.

Cut a piece of cardboard 1/2 inch (1cm) longer than the desired length of the tassel. Wrap yarn around the cardboard 20 times for tassels shorter than 2 inches (5cm). Wrap yarn 30 or more times for longer tassels. These numbers are just guidelines. Skinny tassels need fewer windings than fat ones.

Thread a doubled piece of yarn in a broad-eye needle. Run the needle and yarn between the cardboard and

looped yarn. Tie together both ends of the piece of yarn. Later use this piece of yarn to sew the tassel to the garment. Cut through the wound yarn at the bottom of the cardboard. This allows cardboard to fall out.

Wind a piece of yarn around the tassel about 1/2 inch (1cm) from the top. Wind it around two or three times. Knot ends together tightly. Trim ends close to the knot, and tuck them into the tassel. Trim the bottom edge of tassel so it's even.

Adding Elastic Thread—To make a garment fit better, elastic thread may be added to the waist and cuff. Elastic thread comes in white and black. If either of these colors matches your garment, work it along with your regular yarn.

If the color is noticeable, weave the elastic into the completed garment on the wrong-side. Using an embroidery needle, weave elastic thread into the *back* of the stitches.

DUPLICATE-STITCHING

You may have seen pictures knitted into sweaters. They are made by changing yarn colors according to a given chart. A sweater may be used like a painting canvas, or it may serve as a background for animals or other motifs. *Duplicate-stitching* is a simple way to achieve the same effect. You can see a chart on page 73 for duplicate-stitching the letter in the *Varsity-Letter Sweater,*

How to Work Duplicate-Stitching—Duplicate-stitching is usually done over stockinette stitch. Use yarn in a different color, but of the same weight or heavier, than the garment background.

Stitching Method—Thread an embroidery or tapestry needle with the desired yarn. Secure the yarn at the back of the garment. Bring the yarn to the front through the center of the stitch where you want to begin.

Insert the needle at the top-right corner of the stitch. Bring it behind to the top-left corner of the same stitch, through to the front. See illustration below.

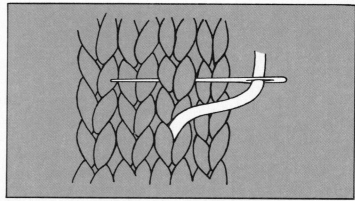

Insert needle at top-right corner of stitch.

Insert the needle at the bottom of the stitch where you started. Pull the yarn to the back again. Continue this for every stitch, according to a picture chart you select.

Suggested Uses—Here are some suggestions for using duplicate-stitching to create different designs:

- Duplicating chart for knitted-in designs.
- Personalizing garments with monograms.
- Adding geometric lines across, up and down, or along the diagonal.

1. Wind yarn around cardboard.

2. Thread yarn through broad-eye needle. Pass it between cardboard and looped yarn.

3. Wind piece of yarn around tassel 1/2 inch from top.

4. Trim bottom edges of tassel so it's even.

- Making fake argyle patterns.
- Creating your own designs. Designs may be done on graph paper. Make geometrics, such as letters, crosses or arrows, or pictures, such as hearts, shamrocks and animals.

Graph-Paper Method — You can draw designs on ordinary graph paper. Choose graph paper with the width of each square about the same size as a stitch in your knitting. One square inch of knitting has more rows than stitches. Outline your design in the width you want. Make the height of the design about 1/3 longer than you want. Make a duplicate-stitch on the sweater for every square within the outline.

You can buy graph paper specially proportioned for knitting stitches. This is easier to use than ordinary graph paper. You can chart a design in the exact size and you don't have to elongate the height. The *Buyer's Guide,* page 128, lists one supplier of this kind of graph paper.

COMPUTERIZED PATTERNS

Some yarn shops offer personal service by adapting existing pattern instructions to suit you. This might mean changing the size of a pattern to fit your figure, substituting another stitch pattern or accommodating other requirements.

Some stores now offer computerized knitting instructions. Here is a brief explanation how a computer works in this situation. You begin by asking someone at a knitting store to adapt an existing pattern to your size or create a new pattern. They ask you to specify the shape, such as neckline or sleeve length, appropriate measurements and desired stitch pattern.

In the traditional method, the knitting expert calculates appropriate instructions and writes them on a piece of paper. This process can take from 5 to 20 minutes.

With a computer, you supply the same information, and the calculation time is reduced to about 2 minutes. The operator feeds the information into the computer, the computer calculates it and your personal pattern is printed out.

The computer can calculate the required number of stitches for a new gauge if you want to use a heavier yarn than specified in a pattern. If a sweater is shown in women's size only, but you want to knit "his" and "hers," the computer can work out a man's size.

A store decides whether to provide personalized instructions by mental calculation or computer. Either way should be satisfactory to you.

MACHINE KNITTING

Most hand knitters know little about knitting machines. Below is some information about them.

Speed — Usually your first thought about knitting machines is they are faster. It takes about two to three hours to complete a long-sleeve sweater, but a certain amount of initial setting-up time is required.

Learning — Manufacturers say operation of a knitting machine is simple, but you don't just sit down and begin knitting. To understand what is involved, watch someone at work. If possible, try some simple procedures yourself. In the beginning, most people benefit from the guidance of an experienced operator.

Appearance — Garments knitted on machines have an even-looking appearance. All stitches are alike. Hand-knitted sweaters look handcrafted. If you use a knitting machine, you sacrifice the uneven texture of hand knitteds.

Patterns — There are knitting-machine patterns for all types of garments. Complex argyles and other designs are not difficult to make on a knitting machine.

Yarns — Most machines use sport-weight or finer yarns. They may also work with worsted-weight yarn. Machines for working with bulky yarns are also available.

Production Craft — Machine knitting is most valuable if you wish to knit more than one garment of the same kind. You can increase your production, but consider whether you have the need. This may be a viable purchase if you want to sell your work.

A knitting machine may be for you if you like to see quick results. You may want one if you like designs with many colors and stitch variations or if you enjoy working out your own patterns. A knitting machine could be useful if you want to make many knitted garments.

Additional Information — *Machine Knitters News* and *Machine Knitting Newsletter* are two publications that offer you sources and resources in the field.

SIZE CHART

Body and chest measurements	20 (51	21 54	22 56	23 59	24 26 61 66	28 30 71 76	31 32 79 82	34 87	36 92	38 97	40 42 102 107	44 46 inches 112 117cm)
Infants and Toddlers Size	1	2	3	4								
Children's and Teens Size *Knitted Size*				4 *Small*	6 8 *Medium*	10 12 *Large*						
Women's Size *Knitted Size*						6 *Small*	8 10 *Medium*	12	14 *Large*	16		
Men's Size *Knitted Size*										38 *Small*	40 42 *Medium*	44 46 *Large*

Use this size chart to help you determine the correct size to make.

Sampler of Stitches

It's easy to change the surface texture of a knit garment. All you have to do is arrange knit and purl stitches in different combinations. The surface texture can be rough or smooth, tweedy or lacy.

Nineteen stitch patterns have been selected for use in this book. The basis for selecting stitches was:

- Basic stitches every knitter should know, such as stockinette stitch and ribbing.
- Selection of contrasts in texture and appearance to achieve many looks.
- Simplicity.

ABOUT STITCH SAMPLES

Each stitch pattern is illustrated with a photograph. Instructions for each pattern are given row by row. Read instructions completely before making any test swatches. It may also help to read instructions out loud.

REPEATS

You will find some patterns are preceded by the statement: *Multiple of x stitches, plus y, worked over z rows.*
Multiples—Some stitches within each row repeat themselves. In some patterns, the row is always divisible by a certain number, called a *multiple*. Occasionally odd stitches are placed at the beginning and end of a row. This is specified in the pattern.
Row Repeats—Patterns repeat for a certain number of rows.

INTERCHANGING STITCH PATTERNS

Stitch patterns are usually interchangeable. Some stitch patterns stretch more in one direction than in another and have other characteristics. Each garment or project is shown in a specific stitch. Sometimes alternative stitches that are suitable for a garment are suggested. You will find these suggestions in each pattern, in the *Design Your Own* section.

GARTER STITCH

In garter stitch, *every* stitch in *every* row is a knit stitch. The resulting texture is grainy and bumpy.

This pattern is worked over every row.
Every row: Knit across.

Garter stitch

STOCKINETTE STITCH

Stockinette stitch is one of the most-common stitches used. The name was coined in the days when socks were knitted by hand. The smooth texture of this pattern provided the greatest wearing comfort. Stockinette stitch has more stretch from side to side than from top to bottom.

This pattern is worked over two rows.

Row 1: Knit across row.
Row 2: Purl across row.

Stockinette stitch

REVERSE-STOCKINETTE STITCH

This is worked the same way as stockinette stitch, but the reverse side becomes the right-side.

This pattern is worked over two rows.

Row 1: Purl across row.
Row 2: Knit across row.

Reverse-stockinette stitch

SINGLE RIBBING

Ribbing gives elasticity to knitwear and is used for waists and cuffs. It is also popular for the body of garments. Ribbing is created by alternating knit and purl stitches within a row. Knit stitches sit on top of knit stitches, and purl stitches sit on top of purl stitches.

This pattern is worked in multiples of two.

*Every row: *Knit 1, purl 1; repeat from * across every row.*

Single ribbing

Double ribbing

DOUBLE RIBBING
Double ribbing is used as often as single ribbing. Two knit and two purl stitches alternate.

This pattern is worked in multiples of four.

*Every row: *Knit 2, purl 2; repeat from * across every row.*

Varsity ribbing

VARSITY RIBBING
Ribbing can also be made of an unequal number of stitches. You can make your own combinations, such as knit five, purl two. This could be used for the body of a sporty sweater.

This pattern is worked in multiples of three, over two rows.

*Row 1: *Knit 1, purl 2; repeat from * across row.*
*Row 2: *Knit 2, purl 1; repeat from * across row.*

RIDGE STITCH
Most knitters find knit stitches more fun to work than purl stitches. The ridge stitch is geared to this preference. Several rows of stockinette stitch alternate with an occasional extra row of knit stitch. You can vary the number of rows between the ridges from the sample shown.

This pattern is worked over six rows.

Row 1: Knit across row.
Row 2: Ridge row. Knit across row.
Row 3: Knit across row.
Row 4: Purl across row.
Row 5: Knit across row.
Row 6: Purl across row.

Ridge stitch

SEED STITCH

Seed stitch is also called *moss stitch.* Every row is knit one, purl one across the row. Knit stitches sit on top of purl stitches and vice versa. Work with an uneven number of stitches. When you work the seed stitch, you produce a firm, grainy texture that keeps its shape well.

This pattern is worked in multiples of two, plus one.
Every row: Knit 1, purl 1 across row, end with a knit 1.

Seed stitch

PEBBLE STITCH

Pebble stitch works up faster than seed stitch. The pebbly texture is considered the right-side. The vertical stripe found on the reverse side is also attractive.

This pattern is worked in multiples of two, over two rows.
Row 1: Knit across row.
*Row 2: *Knit 1, purl 1; repeat from * across row.*

Pebble stitch   Reverse side of pebble stitch

SIMPLE-SIMON STITCH

Simple-simon stitch is good to work on while watching television. The knit-three-purl-one repeat on every other row becomes an easy rhythm. A quick glance tells you whether to start a row with knit one or knit three.

This pattern is worked over four rows.
Row 1: Wrong-side. Purl across row.
*Row 2: *Knit 3, purl 1; repeat from *, end with knit 3.*
Row 3: Purl across row.
*Row 4: Knit 1, purl 1, *knit 3, purl 1; repeat from * across row, end with knit 1.*

Simple-simon stitch

Waffle stitch

WAFFLE STITCH

Waffle stitch makes an attractive overall pattern. You can also use it to create a textured yoke or other area accent.

This pattern is worked in multiples of three, over four rows.

*Row 1: *Knit 2, purl 1; repeat from * across row.*
*Row 2: *Knit 1, purl 2; repeat from * across row.*
Row 3: Work same as row 1.
Row 4: Knit across row.

Ribbed lace

RIBBED LACE

A lacy texture is created by wrapping the yarn over the needle and knitting the next two stitches together.

This pattern is worked in multiples of four, plus two, over two rows.

Row 1: Purl across row.
*Row 2: *Knit 2, yarn over, knit 2 together; repeat from * across row, end with knit 2.*

Basket-weave stitch

BASKET-WEAVE STITCH

This pattern looks the same on both sides, which makes it reversible. The sample shown is made of blocks of five stitches and eight rows, but you can increase or decrease this number as you desire.

This pattern is worked in multiples of ten, over eight rows.

*Rows 1 to 4: *Knit 5, purl 5; repeat from * across row.*
*Rows 5 to 8: *Purl 5, knit 5; repeat from * across row.*

BOBBLES

Bobbles look intricate, but once you realize you work several times into one stitch, you're on your way. Bobbles can be used sparingly in occasional rows, as spots or in diagonal lines. Bobbles can also be made in an overall pattern.

The swatch shows a bobbles row separated by seven rows of stockinette stitch. Each bobble is created with three stitches and three turns in each stitch. This will become clear when you try it. You can create smaller bobbles with fewer stitches and fewer turns. Larger bobbles can be made with up to five stitches and five turns on one stitch.

To make each bobble:

Knit 1, yarn over, knit 1, turn to wrong-side. Purl 3, turn to right side. Knit 3, turn to wrong-side. Purl 3, turn to right side. Slip 1, knit 2 together, pass slipped stitch over.

Follow these steps to make a sample swatch 31 stitches wide, with bobbles on every eighth row. The pattern is worked in multiples of four, plus three, over eight rows.

Row 1: Purl across row.
*Row 2: Make bobbles: *Knit 3, make a bobble; repeat from * across row, end with knit 3.*
Rows 3, 5 and 7: Purl across row.
Rows 4, 6 and 8: Knit across row.

Bobbles

BRICK-AND-MORTAR STITCH

In this two-color pattern, the darker color is used for brick and the lighter color for mortar. Begin by casting on with the lighter color.

The pattern is worked in multiples of four, plus three, over eight rows.

Rows 1 and 2: With light color, knit across row.
*Row 3: With dark color, knit 1, *slip 1 as if to knit, with yarn in back, knit 3; repeat from *, end with slip 1, knit 1.*
*Row 4: With dark color, purl 1, *slip 1 as if to to purl, with yarn in front, purl 3; repeat from * across row, end with slip 1, purl 1.*
Rows 5 and 6: With light color, knit across row.
*Row 7: With dark color, knit 3, *slip 1 with yarn in back, knit 3; repeat from * across row.*
*Row 8: With dark color, purl 3, *slip 1 with yarn in front, purl 3; repeat from * across row.*

Brick-and-mortar stitch

Zigzag stitch

ZIGZAG STITCH

Zigzag stitch uses yarn in two colors or two textures. You can see its application in the *Black-and-White Zigzag* sweater, page 83. To create the color change, twist yarns around each other. Pick up the discarded color on the next row. The yarn is carried loosely across the back of the work. After working a few rows on the sample swatch, you'll find this isn't hard to do.

The basic formula is easy to understand. The color change takes place over six stitches. Any number of stitches can be added to obtain the required width. In the instructions for a 30-stitch sample swatch below, 12 stitches of stockinette are added to both sides of the zigzag.

This pattern is worked over four rows.

Row 1: Right-side with color A, knit 18; with color B, knit 12.
Row 2: With color B, purl 15; with color A, purl 15.
Row 3: With color A, knit 12; with color B, knit 18.
Row 4: With color B, purl 15; with color A, purl 15.

Cable stitch

CABLE STITCH

The cable pattern is a favorite with many knitters. The example shown here is one of many variations. You can make narrower or wider cables by changing the number of stitches in the cable.

Directions below explain how to make the actual cable, which is 10 stitches wide. The reverse-stockinette stitch is used on both sides of the cable. This means all rows in knit stitch for the cable are purled for reverse stockinette.

This cable pattern is worked over 10 stitches and 12 rows.

Rows 1, 3 and 5: Knit 10 stitches.
Rows 2, 4 and 6: Purl 10 stitches.
Row 7: Twist row. Slip 5 stitches on a cable needle and hold at the back of the work. Knit 5 stitches, then knit the 5 stitches from the cable needle.
Rows 8, 10 and 12: Purl 10 stitches.
Rows 9 and 11: Knit 10 stitches.

LOOP-DE-DOOP

Even a beginner can work the loop-de-doop stitch. This stitch creates an airy texture on summer sweaters and stoles and on light afghans. Loops are created by wrapping the yarn over the needle between all stitches. On the next row, extra loops are dropped. Loop rows can be placed between rows of garter, stockinette or other stitch patterns.

In the sample swatch, yarn is wrapped around *twice*. It can be wrapped around one or three times for loops of different sizes. In the *Baby Blanket,* page 35, single and double loops alternate.

This pattern is worked over eight rows.

Rows 1 through 6: Knit across each row, making garter stitch.

*Row 7: *Knit 1, wrap yarn around needle twice from front to back; repeat from * across row, end with knit 1.*

*Row 8: *Knit 1, drop loops; repeat from * across row, end with knit 1.*

Loop-de-doop

GIANT DAISY PETALS

Daisy petals look like embroidery, but are actually worked in the knitting. The pattern is worked over eight rows. Six rows are stockinette stitch. Loops for the daisy petals are worked on the other two rows. Long loops are created by making stitches five rows below the current knitting line. This stitch pattern is easy to do after you practice making two or three daisies.

This pattern is worked in multiples of ten, plus five, over eight rows.

Rows 1, 3 and 5: Knit across row.

Rows 2, 4 and 6: Purl across row.

*Row 7: Knit 5, *knit 1, make loop, knit 2, make loop, knit 2, make loop, knit 5; repeat from * across row.*

To make the first loop, count over two stitches to the left and down five rows. Insert the right needle through the center front of this stitch to the back of the work. Loop your working yarn over the needle, keeping yarn very loose. Draw needle and loop of yarn back through the work. Yarn is now a long loop on the right needle. Knit the next two stitches. Make a second loop through the same stitch hole as before. Knit two stitches. Make a third loop through the same stitch hole. After you have pulled a loop through and placed it on the right needle, put the index finger of your left hand in the loop from behind. This allows enough yarn for the petal to lie flat.

*Row 8: *Purl 5, purl 2 together, purl 1, purl 2 together, purl 1, purl 2 together; repeat from *, end with purl 5.*

Giant daisy petals

Accessories and Small Things

Small projects are easy for a beginning knitter to make. They are also fun to do! When you give a small project or accessory as a gift, it shows someone you care about them. Projects can also help you experiment with a new yarn or use yarn left from other projects.

When more than one size is given for a pattern, circle or highlight the column of the size you want to knit. This is described in *Learning to Knit,* page 7.

Super Headband.

SUPER HEADBAND

This headband keeps ears warm and hair from flying in the eyes. It also looks attractive. Make this headband as an accessory to go with a sweater or give one as a special gift.

DESIGN YOUR OWN
Beginner Project—This is a great project for a beginning knitter. To make it even easier, knit the headband in garter stitch.
Size Adjustments—For a custom fit, measure around the wearer's head. Multiply the number of inches by 2-1/2, which is the stitch gauge. Round this up to the next highest number. Cast on that number of stitches. If the head size is 19 inches, then 19 x 2-1/2 = 47-1/2. You would cast on 48 stitches.

SUITABLE YARN
Bulky yarn or other yarn used double

YARN SHOWN
45% wool-55% acrylic thick-thin *Zigana* by Kendex
1-1/4 ounces = 50 grams
88 yards = 80 meters
Color: Blue

TOOLS AND SUPPLIES
No. 10 needles or size to obtain correct gauge

STITCH PATTERN
Ribbing—*Knit 1, purl 1; repeat from * across every row.

GAUGE
2-1/2 stitches = 1 inch (2-1/2cm) approximately
4 rows = 1 inch (2-1/2cm) approximately

SIZE
Head size 21 inches (54cm).

YARN REQUIRED
1 skein

Pattern
Check your gauge to avoid disappointment.

Cast on	52 stitches
Work even in knit-1-purl-1 ribbing for	2 inches (5cm)
Bind off	18 stitches
This leaves	34 stitches
Work even in ribbing pattern for	2 inches (5cm)
Bind off loosely.	

FINISHING
Stitch short ends of headband together to form a circle.

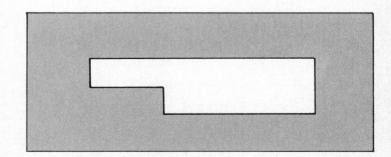

Star Hat.

STAR HAT

The top of this hat looks like a five-point star, but the hat is actually knitted in a rectangle. A star is formed by binding off abruptly and tightly pulling stitches together. This hat is reversible and can be worn pebbly side out one day and ribbed side out the next. Textures are more prominent if you use solid-color yarn, rather than the variegated type shown in the photograph.

DESIGN YOUR OWN
Sizing — The pattern makes an 18-inch (46cm) circumference, but will fit up to 21-inch (54cm) head size comfortably. If you want to change the head size, cast on three stitches for each additional inch (2-1/2cm). For children, cast on three fewer stitches for every inch (2-1/2cm) smaller.

SUITABLE YARN
Bulky yarn or worsted-weight yarn used double

YARN SHOWN
100% orlon-acrylic *Nantuk* by Columbia-Minerva
3-ounce skeins
Color: Scotch heather

TOOLS AND SUPPLIES
No. 9 needles or size to obtain correct gauge

STITCH PATTERN
Pebble Stitch — Repeat these two rows.
Row 1: Knit across row.
Row 2: *Knit 1, purl 1; repeat from * across row.

GAUGE
Worsted-weight yarn, used double:
3 stitches = 1 inch (2-1/2cm)
5 rows = 1 inch (2-1/2cm) approximately

SIZE
Head size 21 inches (54cm).

YARN REQUIRED
2 skeins

Pattern

Check your gauge to avoid disappointment.

Using yarn double, cast on	54 stitches
Work in pebble stitch. Row 1: Knit across row. Row 2: *Knit 1, purl 1, repeat from * across row. Repeat these two rows. Work even in pebble stitch for	9 inches (22cm)
On next pattern-row 1: Knit 2 stitches together across row. This leaves	27 stitches
On next row: Purl 2 stitches together to last stitch. Purl 1 stitch. This leaves	14 stitches
Cut yarn, leaving 15-inch (38cm) tail. Thread yarn through broad-eye needle. Pull needle through all unknit stitches. Draw stitches together tightly and secure end.	

FINISHING
Sew the short ends together in a seam. Arrange top in five sections. Sections appear star shape when hat is not pulled down close to head.

Baby Bootie-Mitts.

BABY BOOTIE-MITTS

Bootie-mitts are designed to save baby's mom the aggravation of looking for a second bootie or mitten. Bootie-mitts can be used to keep baby's feet *or* hands warm. Make them in pairs, threes or fours.

DESIGN YOUR OWN
Ribbon Bows—Add small ribbon bows to cuffs.
Better Fit—Weave elastic thread in the cuffs, so bootie-mitts stay on better.
Changes—Work bootie-mitts in simple-simon or other textured stitch patterns. Add pompons and other decorations.
Use Leftover Yarn—Baby bootie-mitts are great for using leftover yarn.

SUITABLE YARN
Sport-weight yarn

YARN SHOWN
100% orlon-acrylic 3-ply *Supersport* by Red Heart
3-ounce skeins = 85 grams
Color: Lullabye variegated

TOOLS AND SUPPLIES
No. 7 needles or size to obtain correct gauge

STITCH PATTERNS
Stockinette Stitch—Alternate knit and purl rows.
Garter Stitch—Knit every row.

GAUGE
5 stitches = 1 inch (2-1/2cm)
7 rows = 1 inch (2-1/2cm) approximately

SIZE
Up to 6 months, and 6 to 12 months.

YARN REQUIRED
1 skein

Pattern

Check your gauge to avoid disappointment.

	6 months	12 months
Cast on	25	30 stitches
Work even in stockinette stitch	4-1/2 (12	6 inches 15cm)
Change to garter stitch and work even for	1-1/2 (4	1-1/2 inches 4cm)
Bind off loosely.		

FINISHING
Sew long edges together. Place seam in center. Sew across end. Fold down cuff.

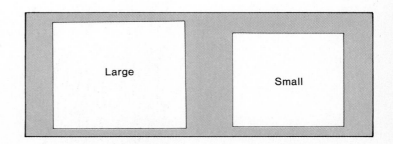

Large

Small

BABY BLANKET

The instructions for this beautiful reversible blanket are easy to follow! It's all in the stitch, which is simple enough for a beginner to work.

DESIGN YOUR OWN
Edging—Crochet around the edges with the same yarn, or pick a yarn in one of the colors in the variegated yarn.
Beribboned—Bind the edges with 2-inch-wide (5cm) blanket binding or ribbon.
Keep Dolly Warm—Knit a doll blanket from leftover yarn.

SUITABLE YARN
Worsted-weight acrylic or wool yarn

YARN SHOWN
100% orlon-acrylic 4-ply by Red Heart
3-ounce skeins = 85 grams
Color: Lullabye variegated

TOOLS AND SUPPLIES
No. 8 needles or size to obtain correct gauge

STITCH PATTERN
Loop-de-doop—Repeat these 16 rows.
Rows 1 through 6: Knit across row.
Row 7: *Knit 1; wrap yarn around needle from front to back; repeat from * across row, end row with knit 1.

Row 8: *Knit 1, drop loop; repeat from * across row; end row with knit 1.
Row 9 through 14: Knit across row.
Row 15: *Knit 1, wrap yarn *twice* around needle from front to back; repeat from * across row; end row with knit 1.
Row 16: *Knit 1, drop loops; repeat from * across row; end row with knit 1.

GAUGE
For garter stitch:
4 stitches = 1 inch (2-1/2cm) approximately

SIZE
32x50 inches (82x128cm).

YARN REQUIRED
7 skeins

Pattern

Check your gauge to avoid disappointment.

Cast on	128 stitches
Knit in loop-de-doop pattern for approximately	50 inches (128cm)
End with row 14 of pattern.	
Bind off loosely.	

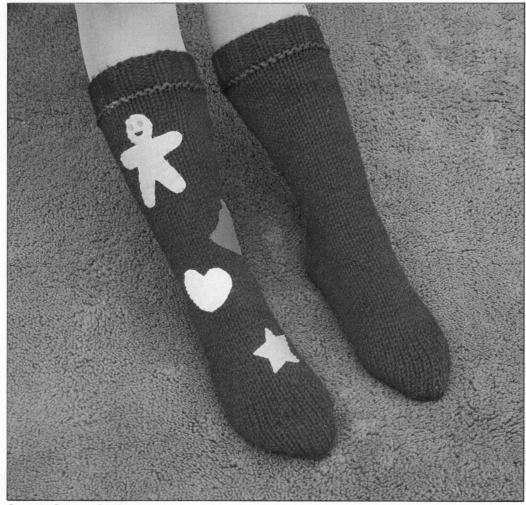

Santa's Slipper Socks.

SANTA'S SLIPPER SOCKS

Hang these socks by the chimney or give a pair to every member of the family. You can wear them all year. These versatile slippers fit foot lengths from 6 to 12 inches (15 to 30cm). The pattern is simple—a plain rectangle knitted in ribbing and stockinette stitch. Rug yarn wears well.

The photo shows a pair of slippers. One sock is plain knitting, without decoration. The other sock shows decorations you can use.

DESIGN YOUR OWN
At No Cost—Make these slippers from leftover yarn of almost any kind. Worsted-weight yarn, used double, works up almost like rug yarn. Make test swatches to get the gauge specified in the pattern. Contrasting trim needs little yarn. You may be able to substitute leftover yarn at all times.

Stripes—Knit the slippers in 1-inch-wide (2-1/2cm) stripes from beginning to end.

Fun Time—Instead of Christmas decorations, make duplicate-stitch hearts. For children, use pompons or attach fringe below the ribbing. Embroider initials or a complete name on a sock.

Protective Soles—In some craft and hobby stores, you can buy moccasin soles, punched with holes. These are ready to be sewn to the bottom of the slippers. It makes them last longer.

SUITABLE YARN
Heavy rug yarn

YARN SHOWN
100% dacron-polyester rug yarn by Red Heart
1-3/5 ounces = 70 yards
Main color: Red
Contrast color: Green

TOOLS AND SUPPLIES
No. 8 needles or size to obtain correct gauge

STITCH PATTERNS
Ribbing—*Knit 2, purl 2, repeat from * across every row.
Stockinette Stitch—Alternate knit rows and purl rows.

GAUGE
3-1/2 stitches = 1 inch (2-1/2cm)
5 rows = 1 inch (2-1/2cm) approximately

SIZE
Small, medium and large for
children and adults.

Length of foot	**Small** 6-8 (15-20	**Medium** 9-10 22-25	**Large** 11-12 inches 28-30cm)
Knitted length	11 (28	14 36	18 inches 46cm)

Yarn required:
  Main color
  Contrast color
	
	2
	1
		
		3
		1
			
			4 skeins
			1 skein

Pattern

Check your gauge to avoid disappointment.

Make two slippers alike. With main color cast on	20	28	36 stitches
Work in knit-2-purl-2 ribbing for	1-1/2 (4	1-1/2 4	1-1/2 inches 4cm)
Change to contrast color. Do not break main-color yarn. Knit across 2 rows. Cut contrast-color yarn. Change to main color and stockinette stitch. Begin with knit row. Work even until total length measures	 9-1/2 (24	 12 30	 15-1/2 inches 39cm)
Decrease 1 stitch at *both* ends of every row, until remain.	6	8	10 stitches
Bind off loosely.			

FINISHING
Fold slipper in half lengthwise. Sew short, tapered
edge together, then sew long edge. Leave other short
edge open.

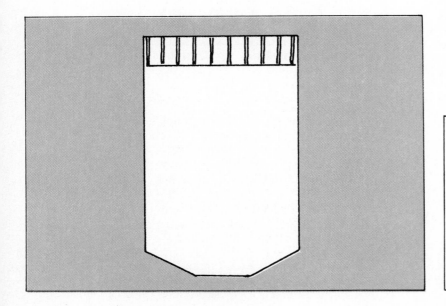

To avoid loose, baggy stitches on
the edges of your work, slip the first
stitch of every row.

A Pair of Potholders.

PAIR OF POTHOLDERS

A potholder is a simple square and makes an ideal project for a beginning knitter. Whether a beginning or advanced knitter, you can turn a potholder into a test for experimenting with new stitch patterns. This test will tell you whether stitches appeal to you before you make a sweater. And you'll make something useful.

Knit a 6-inch (15cm) potholder any way you like. This pattern, with complete step-by-step directions, is an example of what you can invent yourself. Small needles were used to obtain a tight fabric to protect hands.

DESIGN YOUR OWN
Checkerboard—Use two or four colors for the four squares that make up the potholder shown in the photo.
Multiplication Afghan—Knit a lot of potholders without crocheted edgings, sew them together and you have an afghan.
Potpourri—Here's your chance to use odds and ends of cotton yarn. Send potholders instead of greeting cards. Just attach a piece of paper with your message.

SUITABLE YARN
Any cotton yarn

YARN SHOWN
100% cotton *Knit-and-Crochet* by Red Heart
2-1/2-ounce skeins = 70-4/5 grams
Colors: Pink and magenta

TOOLS AND SUPPLIES
No. 4 needles or size to obtain correct gauge
Crochet hook

STITCH PATTERNS
Stockinette Stitch—Alternate knit and purl rows.
Waffle Stitch—Repeat these four rows.
   Row 1: *Knit 2, purl 1; repeat from * across row.
   Row 2: *Knit 1, purl 2; repeat from * across row.
   Row 3: Same as row 1.
   Row 4: Knit across row.

GAUGE
For stockinette stitch:
5 stitches = 1 inch (2-1/2cm)
7 rows = 1 inch (2-1/2cm) approximately

YARN REQUIRED
2 skeins

Pattern

Check your gauge to avoid disappointment.

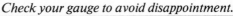

Make four pieces alike, two in each color.

Cast on	30 stitches
Work in waffle pattern for	15 stitches
and in stockinette pattern for	15 stitches
Row 1: *Knit 2, purl 1; repeat from * 4 more times; knit 15.	
Row 2: Purl 15, *knit 1, purl 2; repeat from * 4 more times.	
Row 3: Same as row 1.	
Row 4: Purl 15, knit 15.	
Work even in established pattern for	3 inches (8cm)
End with row 3.	
Next row: Knit across. Reverse block textures. Work stockinette stitch on the first	15 stitches
and waffle pattern on the last	15 stitches
Establish this pattern as follows:	
Row 1: Knit 15, *knit 2, purl 1; repeat from * 4 more times.	
Row 2: *Purl 2, knit 1; repeat from * 4 more times; purl 15.	
Row 3: Same as row 1.	
Row 4: Knit 15, purl 15.	
Work even, repeating 4 pattern rows for	3 inches (8cm)
Bind off loosely in pattern.	

FINISHING
Block potholders. Place two potholders, one of each color, back to back. Crochet around edges once or twice, or sew squares together. End at one corner without breaking yarn. To make a hanger, continue crocheting a single chain for 3 inches (8cm). To form a loop, sew end to corner.

Friendly Monster Puppet.

FRIENDLY MONSTER PUPPET

Anyone can knit this friendly monster hand puppet. The knitted strip is folded and sewn together to show a large red movable mouth.

When basic knitting is finished, the fun begins. Add eyes, ears or any other features. The whole family can offer suggestions, but let everyone knit his or her own puppet.

SUITABLE YARN
Worsted-weight yarn

YARN SHOWN
Worsted-weight yarn in black, gold, peach and red

TOOLS AND SUPPLIES
No. 10 needles or size to obtain correct gauge
Scraps of black and green felt

STITCH PATTERN
Stockinette Stitch—Alternate knit and purl rows. The individual black and gold stripes are knitted unevenly to resemble animal stripes. This is achieved by inserting short rows at random between regular, full-length rows. Beginning at the right edge:
Row 1: Knit across row.
Row 2: Purl across row.
Row 3: Knit halfway across row and turn.
Row 4: Purl back across row.
To begin a short row at the left edge of the work, purl rows 1 and 3, and knit rows 2 and 4.

GAUGE
4 stitches = 1 inch (2-1/2cm) approximately
6 rows = 1 inch (2-1/2cm) approximately

SIZE
Length—16 inches (40cm)
Width—3-1/2 inches (9cm)

YARN REQUIRED
Leftover yarn

Pattern

Check your gauge to avoid disappointment.

With black yarn, cast on	16 stitches
Work in stockinette stitch, for	3-1/2 inches (9cm)
Alternate yellow and black random-width stripes 4 to 6 rows wide. Insert short rows as desired.	
Change to peach color and work even for	2-1/2 inches (6cm)
Change to red color and work even for	4 inches (10cm)
Change to peach color and work even for	2-1/2 inches (6cm)
Work black and yellow stripes for	3-1/2 inches (9cm)
Bind off loosely.	

FINISHING
Fold strip in half across short end. Sew striped side edges together to form short tube. To make mouth, push red section down between the two peach sections. From the side, puppet looks like a Y. See illustrations below. The striped portion forms body. Upper parts are peach outside and red inside. Sew edges of upper parts together. For eyes, cut two small circles from black felt. Sew to one of the peach sections. Cut tongue 2-1/2 inches (6cm) long from green felt. Sew tongue to back of mouth.

TO MAKE PUPPET TALK
Slide thumb into lower part, four fingers into the upper part—and wiggle.

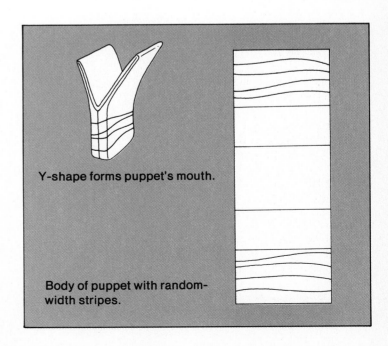

Y-shape forms puppet's mouth.

Body of puppet with random-width stripes.

BABY BUNTING

Tiny face and hands peek out of this cuddly bunting. The peach color complements baby's skin tones. This is an easy-to-make block knit in a basket-weave stitch. Pieces are designed to form a continuous pattern. For this reason, measurements are given in blocks, with inches and centimeters given as an *approximate* check.

DESIGN YOUR OWN
Other Colors—Peach looks nice on a boy or girl, but you may like other colors. Variegated yarns may obscure the distinctive basket-weave pattern.
Other Stitch Patterns—Suitable alternatives include stockinette stitch, simple-simon stitch and pebble stitch.
Contrasting Trim—If you knit with pink, the hood edging and tie can be made with blue. Trim wrist edges and bottom of the bunting with contrasting shade.
Sweater Conversion—Turn the bunting into a sweater by shortening the back and front and omitting the hood. Work the back and front for a total length of 14 blocks, about 9 inches (22cm), or the desired length. Bind off all stitches at the shoulders. Sew together the right shoulder pieces. Leave the center open for the neck opening. Sew two or three small buttons on the left back shoulder. Make corresponding buttonholes with a chain of crochet.
Ribbon Tie—Instead of finishing the hood with crocheting, overcast the edge loosely with an embroidery needle. For the tie, weave a narrow ribbon in and out of the edge.

SUITABLE YARN
Worsted-weight acrylic or wool yarn

YARN SHOWN
100% orlon-acrylic worsted-weight *Softex* by Bucilla
4-ounce skeins = 112 grams
Color: Peach

TOOLS AND SUPPLIES
No. 8 needles or size to obtain correct gauge
1 stitch holder
Large-eye needle
Safety pin
Crochet hook—Suggested size: H

STITCH PATTERN
Basket-Weave Stitch—Repeat these eight rows.
Rows 1 and 3: Knit 5, purl 5 across row.
Rows 2 and 4: Purl 5, knit 5 across row.
Rows 5 and 7: Purl 5, knit 5 across row.
Rows 6 and 8: Knit 5, purl 5 across row.

GAUGE
9 stitches = 2 inches (5cm)
6 rows = 1 inch (2-1/2cm) approximately
3 blocks = 2 inches (5cm) approximately

SIZE
Newborn to 9 months.

Knitted chest measurement	24 inches (61cm)
Underarm sleeve length	6-1/2 inches (16cm)
Length from beginning to shoulder	22 inches (56cm)
Yarn required	3 skeins

Pattern continued on next page.

Pattern

Check your gauge to avoid disappointment.

BACK

Cast on	55 stitches
Work in basket-weave pattern for about	33 blocks 22 inches (55cm)
Shape shoulders by binding off at beginning of next *two* rows	15 stitches
leaving	25 stitches
Work in basket-weave pattern for about	14 blocks 9 inches (22cm)
for total of about	47 blocks 31 inches (79cm)

Bind off loosely in pattern.

FRONT

Cast on	55 stitches
Work in basket-weave pattern for about	29 blocks 19 inches (48cm)
On the next row, divide for neck opening. Work basket-weave pattern over Place them on holder.	27 stitches
On the same row, bind off by passing it over next stitch and dropping it.	1 stitch
Continue working in basket-weave pattern on remaining to complete for total of	27 stitches 4 blocks 33 blocks
Shape shoulder. Bind off at armhole edge	15 stitches
Continue working in basket-weave pattern over remaining for for total of	12 stitches 10 blocks 43 blocks

Bind off loosely.

Place stitches from holder on needle. Needle point is *toward* neck opening. Attach yarn and work in basket-weave pattern over 27 stitches

Continue working this side to match other side.

RIGHT SLEEVE

Cast on	30 stitches
Work in basket-weave pattern for about	12 blocks 8 inches (20cm)

Bind off loosely in pattern, leaving 15-inch (38cm) piece of yarn to sew seam.

LEFT SLEEVE

Cast on	30 stitches

Pattern continued in next column.

Refer to *Stitch Pattern* on page 41, and begin basket-weave pattern with row 5. *Purl 5, knit 5, repeat from * across row. Continue for 12 blocks, same as for right sleeve.

FINISHING

Pieces are designed so basket-weave pattern continues across all seams, with a knit block sewn to purl block. Match block patterns, and sew back and front shoulder seams together. Sew sides of hood together, beginning at shoulders. Back is longer than front, so you'll have four extra lines of blocks on back piece. Sew *sides* of back to top edges of front hood.

Sew sleeves to body of bunting along arm edges. There will be six blocks on either side of shoulder seams. Sew underarm and side seams.

Beginning at bottom of neck, crochet single chain stitch around opening. Work two stitches in each block and one stitch in the bound-off stitch at top of the hood. For tie, crochet chain about 36 inches (92cm) long. Weave chain in and out of crocheted edge with large-eye needle or safety pin. Make a similar edging and tie for bottom of bunting.

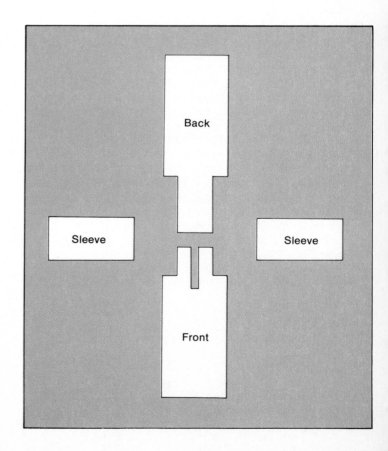

Loopy Afghan.

LOOPY AFGHAN

You may have heard it's the air bubbles in thermal underwear that keep you warm. It's the same with this afghan. Loops help trap the air.

This afghan is a larger version of the baby blanket. In the photo, note the change in texture when knitting is done with a heavier, darker shade of variegated yarn. A slightly different loop-de-doop pattern was also used.

DESIGN YOUR OWN
Fringe—Add fringe along the two shorter edges.
Custom Sizes—Make an afghan any size you like. Decide on the width, then multiply the desired number of inches by 3-1/2, which is the stitch gauge. This will give you the number of stitches to cast on. Knit your afghan to the desired length.

SUITABLE YARN
Worsted-weight wool or acrylic yarn

YARN SHOWN
100% orlon-acrylic 4-ply *Preference* by Red Heart
3-ounce skeins
Color: Mexican variegated

TOOLS AND SUPPLIES
No. 10 circular needle or size to obtain correct gauge

STITCH PATTERN
Loop-de-doop—Repeat these 12 rows.
  Rows 1 to 10: Knit across each row. Makes five ridges.
  Row 11: *Knit 1, wrap yarn around needle *twice* from front to back; repeat from * across row, end with knit 1.
  Row 12: *Knit 1, drop two loops; repeat from * across row; end row with knit 1.

GAUGE
3-1/2 stitches = 1 inch (2-1/2cm) approximately

SIZE
52x68 inches (132x174cm).

YARN REQUIRED
14 skeins

PATTERN

Check your gauge to avoid disappointment.

Cast on	182 stitches
Knit back and forth on circular needle the same way as with straight needles. Do *not* knit around. Work even in loop-de-doop pattern for	68 inches (174cm)
End with row 10 of pattern.	
Bind off loosely.	

KEN'S SCARF AND BARBIE'S SWEATER

If your child sees you knitting, he or she may want to try it. It's best to start with a small project. The scarf and sweater for Barbie- and Ken-size dolls can help your child discover knitting is fun.

On these first tries, don't insist on perfect work. Barbie and Ken won't mind a dropped or increased stitch.

Ken's Scarf

While working on Ken's scarf, your child will learn to cast on, work the knit stitch, then bind off. Instructions for these procedures are given in the *Learning to Knit* section, page 5. It may be helpful to read them out loud when working with your child.

Use up odd yarn you have left from other projects. Worsted-weight is a good yarn. Have your child use size 6, 7 or 8 needles. Don't worry about gauge.

DESIGN YOUR OWN

Other Stitches—Introduce stockinette and other stitch patterns when you think your child is ready.

Stripes—Show your child how to change yarn colors by following these instructions:

With lighter color, knit 6 rows—3 ridges.
With darker color, knit 6 rows—3 ridges.
With lighter color, knit even for a total length of 12 inches (30cm).
With darker color, knit 6 rows—3 ridges.
With lighter color, knit 6 rows—3 ridges.
Bind off.

SUITABLE YARN
Worsted-weight yarn

TOOLS AND SUPPLIES
No. 6, 7 or 8 needles

STITCH PATTERN
Garter Stitch—Knit every row.

GAUGE
Unimportant

YARN REQUIRED
Leftover yarn

PATTERN FOR KEN'S SCARF

Cast on	6 stitches
Work even in garter stitch for	14 inches (36cm)
Bind off all stitches.	

Barbie's Sweater

Knitting a sweater for Barbie or Ken helps your child learn basic procedures.

DESIGN YOUR OWN
Other Sizes—Your child can knit this sweater for larger dolls. To find out how many stitches to cast on, measure the doll around the chest. Divide the number of inches in half to arrive at the measurement for the back or front. Multiply this number by the stitch gauge.

SUITABLE YARN
Worsted-weight yarn

TOOLS AND SUPPLIES
No. 8 needles or size to obtain correct gauge

STITCH PATTERNS
Garter Stitch—Knit every row.
Stockinette Stitch—Alternate knit and purl rows.

GAUGE
4 stitches = 1 inch (2-1/2cm) approximately
6 rows = 1 inch (2-1/2cm) approximately

YARN REQUIRED
Leftover yarn

PATTERN FOR BARBIE'S SWEATER
Check your gauge to avoid disappointment.

BACK

Cast on	12 stitches
Work in garter stitch for	2 rows
Change to stockinette stitch and work even for total length of	1-1/2 inches (4cm)
At beginning of next cast on for total of	2 rows 6 stitches 24 stitches
Work even for	1-1/4 inches (3cm)
Bind off all stitches.	

FRONT
Work front same as back.

FINISHING
Sew top of sleeves together. Leave center-neck opening of 2 inches (5cm). Sew underarm and side seams.

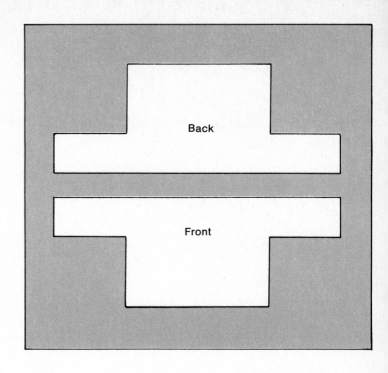

Canine Coat.

CANINE COAT

Your dog is also a family member, so knit a sweater to keep him or her cozy on a cold day. Instructions are given for a size to fit a small dog. You'll find information about adapting the pattern for the correct size to fit your family pet.

SUITABLE YARN
Worsted-weight acrylic or wool yarn

YARN SHOWN
100% acrylic *Windrush* by Brunswick
3-ounce skeins = 100 grams
Color: Persimmon
100% acrylic *Nantuk* by Columbia Minerva
3-ounce skeins
Color: Copperglow

TOOLS AND SUPPLIES
No. 8 needles or size to obtain correct gauge
A few inches of Velcro or other touch-and-close tape

STITCH PATTERNS
Ribbing—*Knit 1, purl 1; repeat from * across every row.
Pebble Stitch—Repeat these two rows.
Row 1: *Knit 1, purl 1; repeat from * across row.
Row 2: Knit across row.

GAUGE
9 stitches = 2 inches (5cm)
6 rows = 1 inch (2-1/2cm) approximately

SIZE
Knitted Measurements—The following measurements are for a small dog:
Length, with cuff turned over—13 inches (33cm).
Width, excluding straps—10 inches (25cm).
Make a Coat to Fit Your Dog—For the width, measure from shoulder to shoulder on your dog. Multiply the number of inches by the number of stitches in the gauge. This gives you the number of stitches to cast on. For the length, measure from the neck to the tail of your dog. Add 1 inch (2-1/2cm) to make a turned-over cuff.

For length of straps, first knit the main body. Place it on your dog, and measure the uncovered space across the neck and belly. Add 1 inch (2-1/2cm) to these measurements for overlapping closures. Make straps this length.

YARN REQUIRED
2 skeins

Pattern

Check your gauge to avoid disappointment.

MAIN BODY	
With light-color yarn, cast on or number of stitches required for correct size.	44 stitches
Work in knit-1-purl-1 ribbing for	1-1/2 inches (4cm)
Change to dark-color yarn, but do not break light-color yarn. Work in pebble stitch, beginning with a knit-1-purl-1 row. Work even for	4 rows
Cut dark-color yarn. Carry up lighter color. Work even in light-color yarn in pebble stitch until total length measures or desired length, *less* 1 inch (2-1/2cm).	12 inches (30cm)
Change to knit-1-purl-1 ribbing. Continue with light-color yarn. Work even for	8 rows
Change to dark-color yarn. Work even for Bind off loosely.	4 rows
STRAPS Knit two straps alike.	
With darker color, cast on	7 stitches
Work even in pebble stitch for or desired length, plus 1 inch (2-1/2 cm).	9 inches (22cm)
Bind off loosely.	

FINISHING
Make cuff by folding over bound-off edge 1 inch (2-1/2cm). Sew it down. Sew straps to one long edge of body: one at the cuff and one between front and back legs. Cut Velcro the width of straps. Sew one part of tape to end of each strap. Sew other part to coat to fit your pet.

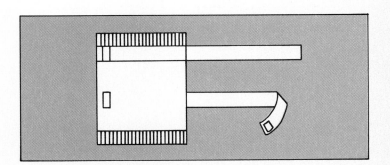

New Classics

New Classics are what they promise—sweaters, jackets and other garments that will stay in your wardrobe for years. Yet they're easy to knit. Most knitters look for this combination—easy to knit with classic lines.

When more than one size is given for a pattern, circle or highlight the column of the size you want to knit. This is described in *Learning to Knit,* page 7.

Simply Striped Sweater.

SIMPLY STRIPED

Don't let the fancy stripes fool you—this is a practical crewneck sweater, in sizes for him or her. Use the colors shown or substitute your own. You can even make this sweater one color.

Fantacia is a thick-and-thin yarn that produces a slightly uneven, appealing texture. This pattern can also be knitted in other types of yarn.

DESIGN YOUR OWN
Basketful of Yarn—This is a good pattern for using leftover yarn. Be sure colors blend well together and knit to the correct gauge. You may be able to use thinner yarns by working them double.

Depending on the quantities of yarn available, you might do the back and front in one color. Stripe only the sleeves.

SUITABLE YARN
Sport-weight acrylic, wool or blended yarn
Color A is used for ribbing and narrow stripes between wider stripes. Contrasting colors are B, C and D.

YARN SHOWN
60% wool-20% silk-20% linen *Fantacia* by Joseph Galler

150 yards = 50 grams
Color A: Beige
Color B: Brown
Color C: Salmon
Color D: Medium blue

TOOLS AND SUPPLIES
No. 4 and No. 6 needles or sizes to obtain correct gauge
1 stitch holder

STITCH PATTERNS
Ribbing—In color A: *Knit 2, purl 2; repeat from * across every row.
Stockinette Stitch—With the color-change sequence shown below, alternate knit and purl rows.
   Color B: 24 rows
   Color A: 6 rows
   Color C: 24 rows
   Color A: 6 rows
   Color D: 24 rows
   Color A: 6 rows

GAUGE
With larger needles, in stockinette stitch:
5-1/2 stitches = 1 inch (2-1/2cm)
8 rows = 1 inch (2-1/2cm) approximately

SIZE
Women's and men's sizes.

	WOMEN			MEN		
	Small	Medium	Large	Small	Medium	Large
Body chest measurements	30-31 (76-79	32-34 82-87	36-38 92-97	38-40 97-102	42-44 107-112	46 inches 117cm)
Knitted chest measurements	33 (84	36 92	39 100	41 104	45 115	48 inches 122cm)
Width of knitted front and back	16-1/2 (42	18 46	19-1/2 50	20-1/2 52	22-1/2 57	24 inches 61cm)

Size continued on next page.

Simply Striped	WOMEN			MEN		
	Small	Medium	Large	Small	Medium	Large
Sleeve length—wrist to underarm	17 (43	18 46	18-1/2 47	19 48	19-1/2 50	21-1/2 inches 55cm)
Length from beginning to shoulder	21 (54	22 56	23 59	24-1/2 62	26-1/2 67	28-1/2 inches 72cm)
Yarn required:						
Color A	3	3	3	4	4	4 skeins
Color B	2	2	2	3	3	3 skeins
Color C	2	2	2	3	3	3 skeins
Color D	2	2	2	3	3	3 skeins

Pattern
Check your gauge to avoid disappointment.

	Small	Medium	Large	Small	Medium	Large
BACK With smaller needles and color A, cast on	84	94	102	108	120	128 stitches
Work in knit-1-purl-1 ribbing for	2-1/2 (6	2-1/2 6	2-1/2 6	3 8	3 8	3 inches 8cm)
On final row of ribbing, increase evenly spaced across row for total of	6 90	6 100	6 108	4 112	4 124	4 stitches 132 stitches
Change to larger needles and stockinette stitch. Begin striped color sequence with color B. Work even for total length of or desired length to shoulder.	21 (54	22 56	23 59	24-1/2 62	26-1/2 67	28-1/2 inches 72cm)
On next right-side row, bind off for shoulder	26	29	31	32	36	39 stitches
Place on holder for back of neck	38	42	46	48	52	54 stitches
Bind off for other shoulder remaining	26	29	31	32	36	39 stitches
FRONT Work front same as back until total length measures	18 (46	19 48	20 51	20-1/2 52	22-1/2 57	24-1/2 inches 62cm)
or less than total desired length to shoulder by	3 (8	3 8	3 8	4 10	4 10	4 inches 10cm)
Begin to shape neck. On next right-side row, knit	32	35	37	40	44	47 stitches
Place on holder for neck Attach yarn. Knit remaining stitches.	26	30	34	32	36	38 stitches
Work both shoulders simultaneously. Decrease 1 stitch every knit row at *both* neck edges for total of remaining on each shoulder.	6 26	6 29	6 31	8 32	8 36	8 times 39 stitches
Bind off loosely in pattern.						
SLEEVES Make two sleeves alike.						
With smaller needles and color A, cast on	42	44	48	54	60	64 stitches

Pattern continued on next page.

Simply Striped	WOMEN			MEN		
	Small	**Medium**	**Large**	**Small**	**Medium**	**Large**
Work in knit-1-purl-1 ribbing for	2-1/2 (6	2-1/2 6	2-1/2 6	3 8	3 8	3 inches 8cm)
On final row of ribbing, increase evenly spaced across row	8	8	10	10	12	12 stitches
for total of	50	52	58	64	72	76 stitches
Change to larger needles and stockinette stitch. Begin striped color sequence with color B. Increase 1 stitch at *both* ends of the row every 1 inch (2-1/2cm)	13	14	15	15	16	16 times
for total of	76	80	88	94	104	110 stitches
Work even until total length measures	17 (43	18 46	18-1/2 47	19 48	19-1/2 50	21-1/2 inches 55cm)
or desired length of sleeve.						
Bind off loosely in pattern.						

FINISHING
Sew right shoulder seam only. For neckband, with smaller needles and right-side of work facing you, attach yarn. Pick up

	WOMEN			MEN		
from left neck edge	16	16	16	22	22	22 stitches
from front holder	26	30	34	32	36	38 stitches
from right neck edge	16	16	16	22	22	22 stitches
from back holder	38	42	46	48	52	54 stitches
for total of	96	104	112	124	132	136 stitches
Work in knit-1-purl-1 ribbing for	1 (2-1/2	1 2-1/2	1 2-1/2	1 2-1/2	1 2-1/2	1 inch 2-1/2cm)

Bind off loosely in pattern.

Sew left shoulder and neckband seam. Set in sleeves. Sew underarm and side seams.

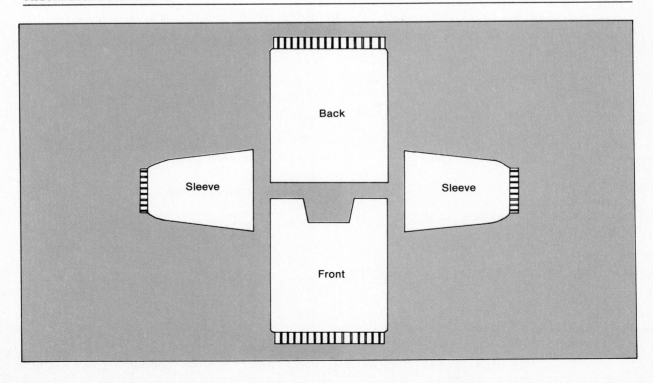

Short Vest.

SHORT VEST

This vest is quick and easy to make. You'll love to wear it when there's a chill in the air or when you want to keep your back warm in front of a fire.

The open front of this short vest makes it comfortable to wear for most women. The pattern is given in one size. Length from waist to shoulder is 16 inches (40cm). To assure a good fit, take a personal measurement and adjust the length if necessary.

This pattern shows how to create a tweed texture by knitting together two yarns of different colors. It also shows how to produce a brushed-yarn effect from regular yarn by brushing the finished garment with a stiff hairbrush.

DESIGN YOUR OWN

Make an Outfit—Knit a long scarf in one of the colors used for the vest. With the second color, duplicate-stitch zigzag stripes near both ends of the scarf.

SUITABLE YARN

Sport-weight yarn, used double, bulky yarn or mohair yarn

YARN SHOWN

100% orlon-acrylic *Fore-'n-Aft Sport* by Brunswick
1-3/4-ounce skeins = 50 grams
Colors: Jade heather and teal

TOOLS AND SUPPLIES

No. 10 needles or size to obtain correct gauge

STITCH PATTERNS

Ribbing—*Knit 1, purl 1; repeat from * across every row.
Stockinette Stitch—Alternate knit and purl rows.

GAUGE

3 stitches = 1 inch (2-1/2cm)
4 rows = 1 inch (2-1/2cm) approximately

SIZE

One size fits all.

Body chest measurements	32-38 inches (82-97cm)
Knitted chest measurements	38 inches (97cm)
Width of knitted back	19 inches (48cm)
Length from waist to shoulder	16 inches (40cm)
Yarn required Total	2 skeins of each color 4 skeins

Pattern continued on next page.

Pattern

Check your gauge to avoid disappointment.

BACK

Using two yarns together, cast on	58 stitches
Work in knit-1-purl-1 ribbing for	3 rows
Change to stockinette stitch. Work even for total length of	8 inches (20cm)
or desired length to armhole.	
Shape armhole by binding off at beginning of next *two* rows.	7 stitches
This leaves	57 stitches
Work even for	8 inches (20 cm)
for total length of	16 inches (40cm)
or desired length.	
Bind off loosely.	

LEFT FRONT

Using two yarns together, cast on	28 stitches
Work in knit-1-purl-1 ribbing for	3 rows
Change to stockinette stitch. Work even for total length of	8 inches (20cm)
or desired length to armhole.	
Shape armhole by binding off at beginning of next knit row.	7 stitches

Pattern continued in next column.

This leaves	21 stitches
Work even for	3-1/2 inches (9cm)
for total length of	11-1/2 inches (29cm)
To shape neck, on next knit row, work to last 3 stitches. Knit 2 together, knit 1. Decrease 1 stitch in the same way on every knit row	8 more times
This leaves	12 stitches
Work even until front measures same as back.	
Bind off loosely.	

RIGHT FRONT

Work right front same as left front, but reverse shaping. Make neck decreases at beginning of knit rows as follows: Knit 1, slip 1, knit 1 and pass slipped stitch over.

FINISHING

Sew shoulders together, and sew side seams. Make row of single crochet around both fronts, the neck and both armholes.
Optional: Press vest with cool iron. To make fuzzy texture, brush with stiff hairbrush. Experiment on your test-gauge swatch to see if you like the effect.

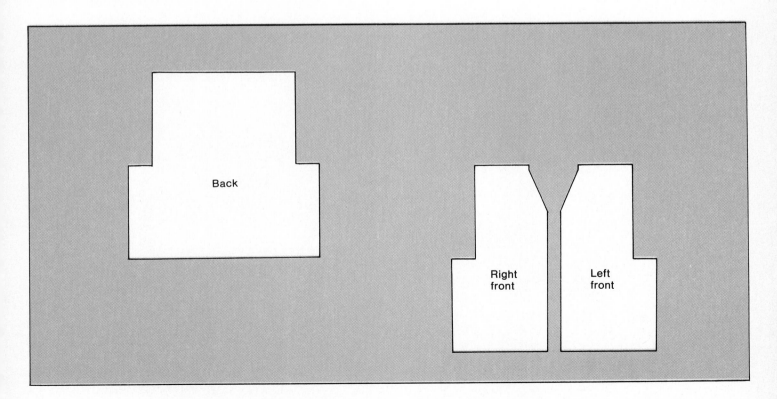

Back

Right front

Left front

RIBBED TURTLENECK

This sweater can be worn alone or layered under shirts. It's sure to become one of your favorites. The body of the sweater is ribbed so it fits well. Two sizes are given to fit most adults and teenagers. Determine the correct size by selecting the measurement closest to actual body measurements. Knitted chest measurements are not specified for this sweater. Flexible sizing is a plus when you knit for someone far away whose measurements you can't check.

DESIGN YOUR OWN

Shoulder Seaming—Because of the bulkiness of ribbing, seam the shoulders with the knitting-together method. See page 16. This results in a smoother seam. For this purpose, place shoulder stitches on holders instead of binding them off.

Color—Knit sweaters in the same color for adult members of the family. Or vary colors to suit individual tastes.

Boat Neck—Change to a boat neckline by omitting the turtleneck. When you reach the shoulder line on the back and front, bind off straight across all stitches. Sew shoulders together. Leave an opening in the center large enough to slip the sweater comfortably over the head.

Short Sleeves—With smaller needles, cast on 76 stitches for the smaller size or 94 stitches for the larger size. Work ribbing for 1 inch (2-1/2cm) before changing to larger needles. Work even in ribbing for 8 inches (20cm) or desired length of sleeve.

SUITABLE YARN

Worsted-weight acrylic, wool or cotton yarn

YARN SHOWN

100% wool worsted *Germantown* by Brunswick
3-1/2-ounce skeins = 220 yards
Color: Cinnamon

TOOLS AND SUPPLIES

No. 6 and No. 8 needles or sizes to obtain correct gauge

STITCH PATTERN

Ribbing—*Knit 2, purl 2; repeat from * across every row.

GAUGE

With larger needles, measured on slightly stretched knitting:
5 stitches = 1 inch (2-1/2cm) approximately
6 rows = 1 inch (2-1/2cm) approximately

SIZE

Women's small-medium and large, and men's small-medium.

Helpful Hint

Some knitters use a circular needle for working neckbands.

	Women's Small-Medium	Women's Large & Men's Small-Medium
Body chest measurements	30-36 (75-92	38-44 inches 97-112cm)
Sleeve length—wrist to underarm	18 (46	20 inches 51cm)
Length from beginning to shoulder	22 (56	26 inches 66cm)
Yarn required	5	7 skeins

Pattern

Check your gauge to avoid disappointment.

FRONT

With smaller needles, cast on	88	96 stitches
Work in knit-2-purl-2 ribbing for	2 (5	2 inches 5cm)
Change to larger needles and continue in ribbing for total length of	22 (56	26 inches 66cm)
or desired length to shoulder.		
For right shoulder, bind off	24	26 stitches
Work center in ribbing for	40	44 stitches
For left shoulder bind off	24	26 stitches

Ribbed Turtleneck.

Pattern continued on next page.

Ribbed Turtleneck	**Women's Small-Medium**	**Women's Large & Men's Small-Medium**
For turtleneck, change to smaller needles. Attach yarn to beginning of center stitches. Work center ribbing for or	40 6 (15	44 stitches 6 inches 15cm)
Bind off loosely in pattern.		
BACK Work back same as front.		
SLEEVES With smaller needles, cast on	40	50 stitches
Work in knit-2-purl-2 ribbing for	2 (5	2 inches 5cm)
Change to larger needles and continue in ribbing. Increase 1 stitch at *both* ends of the needle every 4th row for total of	18 76	22 times 94 stitches
Work even until length of sleeve measures or desired length.	18 (46	20 inches 51cm)
Bind off loosely in pattern.		
FINISHING Sew shoulders together, and sew sides of turtleneck. Set in sleeves. Stretch sleeve ribs at both sides of shoulder seams to at least Sew side and underarm seams.	7-1/2 (19	9-1/2 inches 24cm)

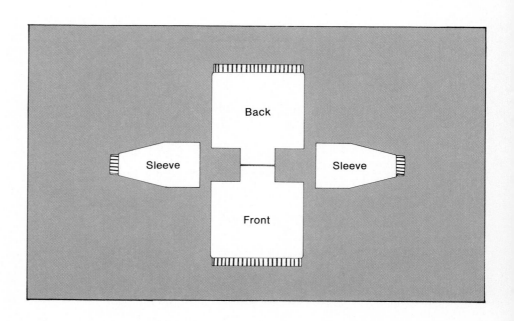

Child's Jacket.

CHILD'S JACKET

Here's an easy knit—it's all done in garter stitch. Sleeves are knitted as part of the back and fronts. The jacket is designed to grow with your child. Sleeves are first turned up as a cuff, then turned down as the child grows.

The pattern shows two useful knitting methods. This first is knitting from sleeve to sleeve, which you might call *sideways.* The second is creating vertical stripes without having to carry different-color yarns up row by row.

In this sweater, two colors are used for the stripes on the sleeves and on the front. Make all the stripes the same color if you prefer. You will find more color ideas in *Design Your Own* below.

DESIGN YOUR OWN

Stripes All Over—Change the color of the stripes. Knit 1-inch-wide (2-1/2cm) stripes across the whole jacket. Plan colors ahead.

Random Stripes—Gather leftover yarn, select ones that go well together, then knit random stripes. It usually works well. Make sure yarns work to the same gauge.

SUITABLE YARN

Worsted-weight acrylic or wool yarn

YARN SHOWN

100% orlon-acrylic *Nantuk* by Columbia-Minerva
4-ounce skeins
Colors: Yellow, dark coral-red and royal blue

TOOLS AND SUPPLIES

No. 9 needles or size to obtain correct gauge
1 separating zipper to fit front

STITCH PATTERN

Garter Stitch—Knit every row.

GAUGE

4 stitches = 1 inch (2-1/2cm)
8 rows (4 ridges) = 1 inch (2-1/2cm) approximately

SIZE

Children's small and medium.

	Small	Medium
Body chest measurements	22-23 (56-59	24-25 inches 61-64cm)
Knitted chest measurements	24 (61	26 inches 66cm)
Width of knitted front	12 (30	13 inches 33cm)

Size continued on next page.

Helpful Hint

Color accents can be achieved by crocheting one or two rows around necklines, wrists, bottom edges and over armhole seams. Use contrasting colors or darker shades of the same yarn.

Child's Jacket	Small	Medium
Sleeve length—wrist to underarm	11 (28	12 inches 30cm)
Total length from waist to shoulder	14 (36	16 inches 40cm)
Yarn required for both sizes:		
Yellow	2	2 skeins
Red	1	1 skein
Blue	1	1 skein

Pattern

Check your gauge to avoid disappointment.

SLEEVES AND BACK

This piece is knitted from wrist to wrist.		
With blue yarn, cast on	16	18 stitches
Work even in garter stitch for 3 inches (8cm).		
Change to yellow yarn. Work even for	7 (18	8 inches 20cm)
for total length of	10 (25	11 inches 28cm)
or 1 inch (2-1/2 cm) more than desired length to underarm.		
Cast on	40	42 stitches
for total of	56	64 stitches
Work even for	12 (30	13 inches 33cm)
Bind off	40	42 stitches
This leaves for sleeve. Be sure sleeves are on same edge of work.	16	18 stitches
Work even for	7 (18	8 inches 20cm)
or to match other sleeve.		
Change to red yarn. Work even for	3 (8	3 inches 8cm)

Bind off loosely.

SLEEVES AND FRONTS

These pieces are knitted from wrist to center front. Right and left fronts are worked alike, except color stripes are reversed as follows: One front, begin at wrist with blue and end at center front with red. Other front, begin at wrist with red and end at center front with blue.

With blue or red cast on	16	18 stitches
Work in garter stitch for 3 inches (8cm).		
Change to yellow. Work even for	7 (18	8 inches 20cm)
for total length of	10 (25	11 inches 28cm)
or same sleeve length as back.		
Cast on	40	42 stitches
for total of	56	64 stitches

Pattern continued on next page.

Child's Jacket	Small	Medium
Work even for	4 (10	4-1/2 inches 12cm)
Shape neck. Bind off at beginning of next row at longer edge	8	8 stitches
This leaves	48	56 stitches
Work even for 1/2 inch (1cm).		
Change to red or blue. Work even for 1-1/2 inches (4cm).		
Bind off loosely.		

FINISHING

Match color bands at wrists. Sew back and front together at sleeves and shoulders. Sew underarm and side seams. Crochet around neck edges.

Use red yarn to crochet from red-center front to center back. Use blue yarn to crochet from blue-center front to center back. Sew in zipper. Turn up cuffs 1 inch (2-1/2cm) or as much as desired.

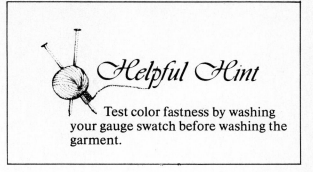

Helpful Hint

Test color fastness by washing your gauge swatch before washing the garment.

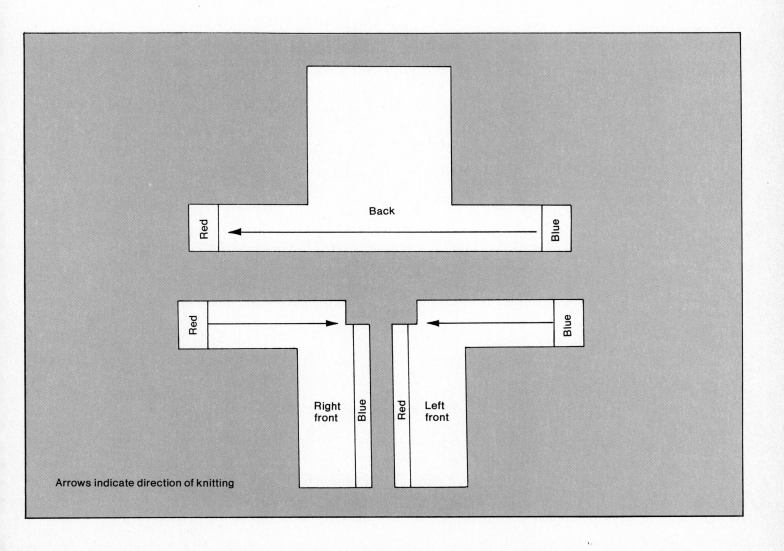

Arrows indicate direction of knitting

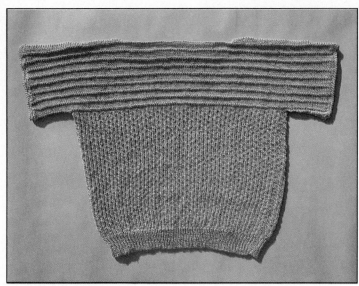

All-Occasion T-Shirt.

ALL-OCCASION T-SHIRT

If you love to wear a T-shirt, this one's for you. It's made of only two pieces—sleeves are worked in one piece with the back and front yokes.

Acrylic yarn and a quick stitch are used so you can make a whole wardrobe in lots of colors. The stitch used is simple-simon stitch—it's simple, fun and easy to do.

DESIGN YOUR OWN
Change the Yoke—Knit the yoke in a different color. The lilac shown would look great with a raspberry or dark-purple yoke. Create a coordinated outfit by matching the yoke color to a favorite skirt or pair of pants.
Crochet Sleeve Edges—With size-C crochet hook, crochet two rows of single crochet around sleeve edges.
Other Stitch Pattern—Knit the main body of T-shirt in seed stitch or other stitch pattern.

SUITABLE YARN
Sport-weight acrylic or cotton yarn

YARN SHOWN
100% acrylic *Luster Sheen* by Red Heart
2-ounce skeins
Color: Lilac

TOOLS AND SUPPLIES
No. 4 and No. 6 needles or sizes to obtain correct gauge

STITCH PATTERNS
Ribbing—*Knit 1, purl 1; repeat from * across every row.
Simple-Simon Stitch—This pattern is worked over a multiple of four, plus three. Repeat the pattern over four rows.
Row 1: Wrong-side. Purl across row.
Row 2: *Knit 3, purl 1; repeat from * across, end with knit 3.
Row 3: Purl across row.
Row 4: Knit 1, purl 1, *knit 3, purl 1: repeat from * across row, end with knit 1.
Ridge Stitch—Repeat this pattern over six rows.
Row 1: Right-side. Knit across row.
Row 2: Knit across the row, to form ridge.
Row 3: Knit across row.
Row 4: Purl across row.
Row 5: Knit across row.
Row 6: Purl across row.

GAUGE
With larger needles, in simple-simon stitch:
6 stitches = 1 inch (2-1/2cm)
8 rows = 1 inch (2-1/2cm) approximately

SIZE
Women's small-medium and large.

	Small-Medium	Large
Body chest measurements	31-34 (79-87	36-38 inches 92-97cm)
Knitted chest measurements	35 (89	39 inches 100cm)
Width of knitted front and back	17 (43	19-1/2 inches 50cm)

Size continued on next page.

All-Occasion T-Shirt	Small-Medium	Large
Sleeve length from wrist to underarm	3 (8	3-1/2 inches 9cm)
Total length	20-1/2 (52	22 inches 56cm)
Yarn required	5	6 skeins

Pattern

Check your gauge to avoid disappointment.

BACK

	Small-Medium	Large
With smaller needles, cast on	98	110 stitches
Work in knit-1-purl-1 ribbing for	2 inches (5	2 inches 5cm)
On final row of ribbing, increase evenly spaced across row for total of	5 103	5 stitches 115 stitches

Change to larger needles and simple-simon stitch.
Row 1: Wrong-side, purl across row.
Row 2: *Knit 3, purl 1, repeat from * across row, end with knit 3.
Row 3: Purl across row.
Row 4: Knit 1, purl 1, *knit 3, purl 1, repeat from * across row, end with knit 1.

	Small-Medium	Large
Work even until total length measures	14 inches (36	15 inches 38cm)

or desired length to underarm.

End with row 2 or 4 of simple-simon pattern.

	Small-Medium	Large
With wrong-side facing you, cast on for sleeve. Purl across row.	18	21 stitches
For other sleeve, cast on for total of	18 139	21 stitches 157 stitches

Begin ridge stitch.
Row 1: Right-side, knit across row.
Row 2: Knit across row.
Rows 3 and 5: Knit across row.
Rows 4 and 6: Purl across row.
Work even in ridge-stitch pattern

until total length measures	20-1/2 (52	22 inches 56cm)

Bind off loosely in pattern.

FRONT
Work front same as back.

FINISHING
Sew shoulders together, leaving 8-inch (20cm) opening for boat neck. Sew side and underarm seams. Turn neck edges under 3/4 inch (2 cm) at center. Taper to nothing at shoulders. Tack edge invisibly to the wrong-side of work.

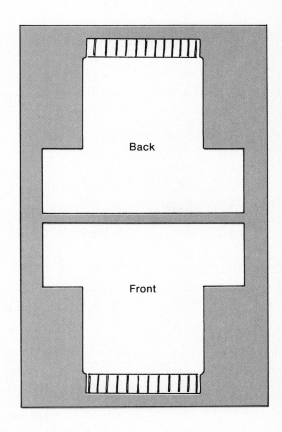

Here-Comes-the-Gang Sweater.

HERE COMES THE GANG

This is an easy pattern to knit in sizes to fit everyone in the family. Waist ribbing is repeated along the neckline and dropped shoulders to give interesting detail to this block knit. This is a loose-fitting sweater. Choose your size with this in mind.

DESIGN YOUR OWN
Color Accent—Work ribbing at the top of all four pieces in a deeper shade of the same color than the rest of the sweater. Or select a contrasting color.

SUITABLE YARN
Worsted-weight acrylic, wool, cotton or mixtures yarn

YARN SHOWN
100% wool *Kerry Donegal Tweed Homespun* by Tahki
176 yards = 100 grams
Color: Dark camel with orange-and-blue flecks

TOOLS AND SUPPLIES
No. 6 and No. 8 needles or sizes to obtain correct gauge

STITCH PATTERNS
Ribbing—*Knit 2, purl 2; repeat from * across every row.
Stockinette Stitch—Alternate rows of knit and purl.

GAUGE
With larger needles in stockinette stitch:
4 stitches = 1 inch (2-1/2cm)
5 rows = 1 inch (2-1/2cm) approximately

SIZE
Complete size range for children, women and men.

	CHILDREN			WOMEN			MEN		
	Small	Medium	Large	Small	Medium	Large	Small	Medium	Large
Body chest measurements	23-24 (59-61	26-28 66-71	30 76	30-31 76-79	32-34 82-87	36-38 92-97	38-40 97-102	42-44 107-112	46 inches 117cm)
Knitted chest measurements	26 (66	29 74	32 82	33 84	36 92	39 100	41 104	45 115	48 inches 122cm)
Width of knitted front and back	13 (33	14-1/2 37	16 40	16-1/2 42	18 46	19-1/2 50	20-1/2 52	22-1/2 57	24 inches 61cm)
Sleeve length—wrist to underarm	11 (28	13 33	15 38	17 43	18 46	18-1/2 47	19 48	19-1/2 50	21-1/2 inches 55cm)
Length from wrist to shoulder	13-1/2 (34	15-1/2 39	17-1/2 44	21 54	22 56	23 59	24-1/2 62	26-1/2 67	28-1/2 inches 72cm)
Yarn required	2	3	4	5	6	7	8	8	9 skeins

Pattern
Check your gauge to avoid disappointment.

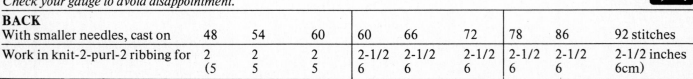

BACK

With smaller needles, cast on	48	54	60	60	66	72	78	86	92 stitches
Work in knit-2-purl-2 ribbing for	2 (5	2 5	2 5	2-1/2 6	2-1/2 6	2-1/2 6	2-1/2 6	2-1/2 6	2-1/2 inches 6cm)

Pattern continued on next page.

Here Comes the Gang	CHILDREN			WOMEN			MEN		
	Small	Medium	Large	Small	Medium	Large	Small	Medium	Large
Change to larger needles and stockinette stitch. On first knit row, increase evenly spaced across row	4	4	4	6	6	6	4	4	4 stitches
for total of	52	58	64	66	72	78	82	90	96 stitches
Work even for total length of	12 (30	14 36	16 40	19-1/2 50	20-1/2 52	21-1/2 55	23 59	25 64	27 inches 69cm)
This is 1-1/2 inches (4cm) less than desired length to shoulder.									
Work in knit-2-purl-2 ribbing for	1-1/2 (4	1-1/2 4	1-1/2 4	1-1/2 4	1-1/2 4	1-1/2 4	1-1/2 4	1-1/2 4	1-1/2 inches 4cm)
Bind off loosely in pattern.									

FRONT
Work front same as back.

SLEEVES

	CHILDREN			WOMEN			MEN		
	Small	Medium	Large	Small	Medium	Large	Small	Medium	Large
With smaller needles, cast on	22	24	26	30	32	32	36	38	40 stitches
Work in knit-2-purl-2 ribbing for	2 (5	2-1/2 6	2-1/2 6	2-1/2 6	2-1/2 6	2-1/2 6	2-1/2 6	2-1/2 6	2-1/2 inches 6cm)
Change to larger needles and stockinette stitch. On first knit row increase evenly spaced across row	2	4	6	4	6	8	4	6	8 stitches
for total of	24	28	32	34	38	40	40	44	48 stitches
Increase 1 stitch at both ends of a knit row every 6th row	6	8	10	11	11	12	12	14	16 times
for a total of	36	44	52	56	60	64	64	72	80 stitches
Work even until sleeve measures	9-1/2 (24	11-1/2 29	13-1/2 34	15-1/2 39	16-1/2 42	17 43	17-1/2 44	18 46	20 inches 51cm)
This is 1-1/2 inches (4cm) less than desired sleeve length. Work in knit-2-purl-2 ribbing for	1-1/2 (4	1-1/2 4	1-1/2 4	1-1/2 4	1-1/2 4	1-1/2 4	1-1/2 4	1-1/2 4	1-1/2 inches 4cm)
Bind off loosely in ribbing.									

FINISHING

	CHILDREN			WOMEN			MEN		
	Small	Medium	Large	Small	Medium	Large	Small	Medium	Large
Sew shoulder seams for about	3 (8	3 8	3 8	4 10	4 10	4 10	5 13	5 13	5 inches 13cm)
Sew in sleeves. Sew underarm and side seam.									

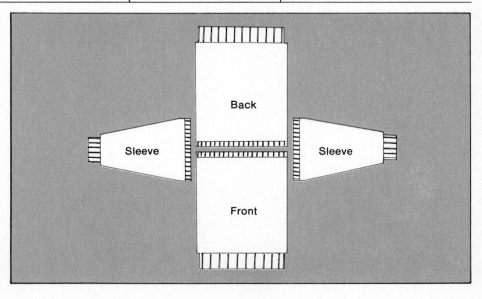

PLAYING WITH BLOCKS

This sweater is simple, smart and versatile. It's a true block knit, worked in four rectangles: back, front and two sleeves. Each stitch is knitted, with no purling. Every two rows form a ridge. Take advantage of this feature by counting ridges to match the length of pattern pieces.

You will find a range of sizes to suit every member of your family. The variety of sizes also helps you select a loose or tight fit, depending on your preference.

DESIGN YOUR OWN

Tunic—Convert this sweater into a longer tunic. Measure from the underarm to the point on the hip where you want the tunic to end. Add the necessary length to the back and front blocks. Leave side seams open about 6 inches (15cm) at the bottom. This procedure is discussed in more detail in the *Designing Your Own* section. See the discussion on page 120.

Longer Sleeves—You may prefer full-length sleeves instead of the three-quarter-length sleeves shown. Add 2 to 3 inches (5 to 8cm) to the specified length of the sleeve.

Stripes—Create 2-inch-wide (5cm) horizontal stripes by changing yarn colors every eight rows. A man might like brown and beige. Children might enjoy teal and yellow or lavender and pink. For random stripes, use variegated yarn.

Another Stitch Pattern—If you prefer, substitute seed stitch for ridge stitch.
Row 1: Knit 1, purl 1 across row.
Row 2: Purl 1, knit 1 across row.

SUITABLE YARN
Worsted-weight acrylic, wool or cotton yarn

YARN SHOWN
100% wool by Candide
4-ounce skein = 190 yards
Color: Horizon blue

TOOLS AND SUPPLIES
No. 10 needles or size to obtain correct gauge

STITCH PATTERN
Garter Stitch—Knit every row.

GAUGE
4 stitches = 1 inch (2-1/2cm)
8 rows = 1 inch (2-1/2cm) approximately
Pieces are usually measured with a tape measure. In garter stitch, you can also count ridges. Two rows of garter stitch create a ridge. In the correct gauge, four ridges equal 1 inch (2-1/2cm).

SIZE
Complete size range for children, women and men.

| | CHILDREN | | | WOMEN | | | MEN | | |
	Small	Medium	Large	Small	Medium	Large	Small	Medium	Large
Body chest measurements	23-24 (59-61	26-28 66-71	30 76	30-31 76-79	32-34 82-87	36-38 92-97	38-40 97-102	42-44 107-112	46 inches 117cm)
Knitted chest measurements	26 (66	29 74	32 82	33 84	36 92	39 100	41 104	45 115	48 inches 122cm)
Width of knitted front and back	13 (33	14-1/2 37	16 40	16-1/2 42	18 46	19-1/2 50	20-1/2 52	22-1/2 57	24 inches 61cm)
3/4-length sleeve, including cuff	11 (28	13 33	15 38	17 43	18 46	18-1/2 47	19 48	19-1/2 50	21-1/2 inches 55cm)
Total length from waist to shoulder	13-1/2 (34	15-1/2 39	17-1/2 44	21 54	22 56	23 59	24-1/2 62	26-1/2 67	29-1/2 inches 75cm)
Yarn required	3	4	5	5	5	6	7	8	9 skeins

Pattern
Check your gauge to avoid disappointment.

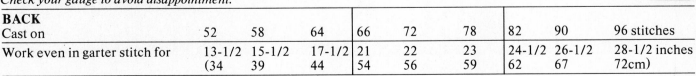

BACK									
Cast on	52	58	64	66	72	78	82	90	96 stitches
Work even in garter stitch for	13-1/2 (34	15-1/2 39	17-1/2 44	21 54	22 56	23 59	24-1/2 62	26-1/2 67	28-1/2 inches 72cm)

Playing-with-Blocks Sweater.

Pattern continued on next page.

Playing with Blocks	CHILDREN			WOMEN			MEN		
	Small	Medium	Large	Small	Medium	Large	Small	Medium	Large
or count ridges	54	62	70	84	88	92	98	106	114 ridges
Bind off loosely.									

FRONT
Work front same as back.

	CHILDREN			WOMEN			MEN		
	Small	Medium	Large	Small	Medium	Large	Small	Medium	Large
SLEEVES Cast on	36	44	52	56	60	64	64	72	80 stitches
Work even in garter stitch for	11	13	15	17	18	18-1/2	19	19-1/2	21-1/2 inches
	(28	33	38	43	46	47	48	50	55cm)
or count ridges	44	52	60	68	72	75	76	78	86 ridges
Bind off loosely in pattern.									
FINISHING Join shoulder seams over	3-1/2	3-1/2	3-1/2	4-1/2	4-1/2	4-1/2	5	5	5 inches
	(9	9	9	12	12	12	13	13	13cm)

Sew in sleeves. Sew underarm and side seams, leaving 4-1/2 inches (12cm) unsewn at waist edges. Turn up sleeve cuffs 2 inches (5cm) for adults, less for children. Tack cuffs to sleeves in two places.

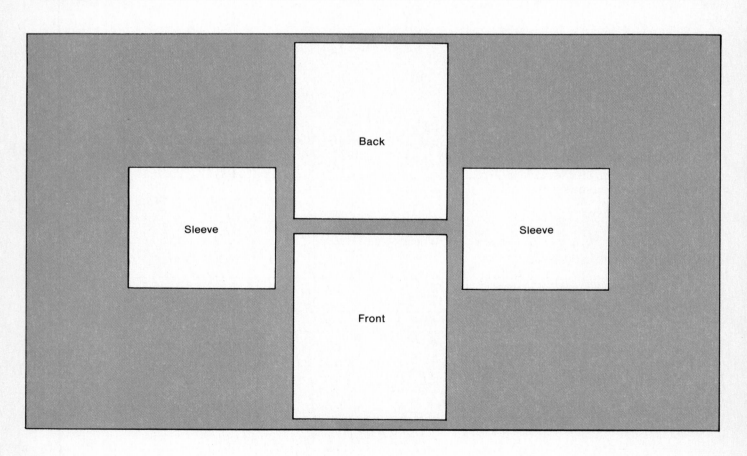

Year-Round Favorite.

YEAR-ROUND FAVORITE

Travelers often have one sweater they always take on a trip. The *Year-Round Favorite* with its placket-neck opening, is a likely candidate for the role. It can be worn alone or layered. Select yarn in a color compatible with your existing wardrobe. Brushed yarn can look sporty or dressy, and it launders well.

The pattern is given in two sizes. You will find only one set of figures, except for the body length and sleeve length. The difference in sizes is controlled by changing needle sizes, rather than changing the number of stitches. This treatment is well-suited to brushed yarns, which expand and contract.

DESIGN YOUR OWN

Sleeve Length—This pattern allows you to determine the length of the sleeve as you work on it. Each sleeve is knitted from the shoulder toward the wrist. You can make short, three-quarter-length or full-length sleeves.

Smooth Shoulders—In this pattern, shoulders look better knitted together, rather than sewn. You will need four additional stitch holders. Do not bind off the 28 stitches for the back and front shoulders. Place them on holders. Knit shoulders together as directed in *Learning to Knit*, page 16.

Button Placket—Add three buttons and buttonholes to the placket. Proceed as follows: From the bottom of the placket on the right front, place first buttonhole up 1-1/2 inches (4cm), second buttonhole up 4 inches (10cm), third buttonhole up 6-1/2 inches (16cm), on neckband. Each buttonhole is made on six center stitches. Reverse procedure for man's sweater.

Row 1: Knit 1, purl 1, knit 2 together, yarn over, knit 1, purl 1.

Row 2: Work in ribbing over six stitches.

Sew buttons on left front to correspond to openings.

Yoke Variation—Create a yoke by starting a different stitch pattern when you begin dividing the front for the placket. Try knit-1-purl-1 ribbing all the way across the row or use seed stitch.

SUITABLE YARN

Worsted-weight yarn or brushed yarn or mohair

YARN SHOWN

50% nylon-50% acrylic *Mirage* by Bucilla
1-3/4 ounces = 50 grams
Color: Banana yellow

TOOLS AND SUPPLIES

For smaller size:
No. 4 and No. 6 needles or sizes to obtain correct gauge
For larger size:
No. 5 and No. 7 needles or sizes to obtain correct gauge
For both sizes:
3 stitch holders
Circular needle in smaller size is recommended for neckband, optional
3 small buttons, optional

STITCH PATTERNS

Ribbing—*Knit 1, purl 1; repeat from * across every row.
Stockinette Stitch—Alternate knit and purl rows.

GAUGE

For smaller size, in stockinette stitch, with larger needles:
5 stitches = 1 inch (2-1/2cm)
7 rows = 1 inch (2-1/2cm) approximately
For larger size, in stockinette stitch, with larger needles:
4-1/2 stitches = 1 inch (2-1/2cm)
6 rows = 1 inch (2-1/2cm) approximately

Pattern continued on next page.

SIZE
Women's small, medium and large. Larger size is large for a woman, small for a man.

	Small-Medium	Large
Body chest measurements	32-34 (82-87	36-38 inches 92-97cm)
Knitted chest measurements	36 (92	40 inches 102cm)
Width of knitted front and back	18 (46	20 inches 51cm)
Sleeve length—underarm to wrist	16 (40	18 inches 46cm)
Length from beginning to shoulder	21 (54	24 inches 61 cm)
Yarn required	6	7 skeins

Pattern

Check your gauge to avoid disappointment.

BACK

With smaller needles, cast on	80 stitches	
Work in knit-1-purl-1 ribbing for	2-1/2 inches (6cm)	
Change to larger needles and stockinette stitch. On first row, increase evenly across row for total of	10 stitches 90 stitches	
Work even for total length of	21 (54	24 inches 61cm)
or desired length to shoulder.		
For shoulder, bind off	28 stitches	
For back neck, place on holder	34 stitches	
For other shoulder, bind off	28 stitches	

FRONT

Work front same as back for	13-1/2 (34	16-1/2 inches 42cm)
or 7-1/2 inches (19cm) less than total desired length.		
Divide for neck placket. On next right-side row, knit	48 stitches	
Place on holder remaining	42 stitches	
For left side, work 6 center stitches in knit-1-purl-1 ribbing and 42 stitches in stockinette stitch.		
Work even in this pattern for	6 inches (15cm)	
Shape neck on next right side row. Knit	28 stitches	
Place on holder	20 stitches	
Work even in stockinette stitch until length matches back.	28 stitches	
Bind off loosely in pattern.		
For right side, attach new yarn and cast on	6 stitches	

Pattern continued on next page.

Year-Round Favorite	Small-Medium	Large
Pick up from holder at center neck and knit for total of	42 stitches 48 stitches	
Work to match left side. Reverse instructions, keeping 6 center stitches in ribbing stitch.		
Sew shoulders together. Tack lower edge of placket to sweater. Mark armholes at side edges of main body with yarn loops 8 inches (20cm) down from shoulder seam, for total armhole length of 16 inches (40cm).		

SLEEVES

	Small-Medium	Large
Pick up at armhole edges, between markers	80 stitches	
Work in stockinette stitch, decreasing at both ends of row every	1 stitch 1 inch (2-1/2cm)	
When total length reaches	16 (40	18 inches 46cm)
decrease evenly across next row until 34 stitches remain.		
Work in knit-1-purl-1 ribbing for	2 inches (5cm)	
Bind off loosely in pattern.		

NECKBAND

	Small-Medium	Large
With smaller size needles, pick up from right-front holder	20 stitches	
from horizontal right neck edge	12 stitches	
from back neck holder	34 stitches	
from horizontal left neck edge	12 stitches	
from left front holder	20 stitches	
for total of	98 stitches	
Work in knit-1-purl-1 ribbing for	1 inch (2-1/2cm)	
Bind off loosely in pattern.		

FINISHING
Sew underarm and side seams.

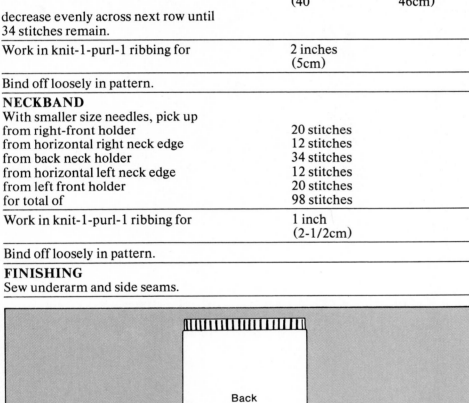

Varsity-Letter Sweater.

VARSITY-LETTER SWEATER

A friend made this sweater for her teenage daughter. The girl's friends were so envious, she allowed some of them to wear it for an hour each.

Work this loose-fitting sweater with your teenager's school colors or someone's college colors. Get the appropriate letter from the school sports department or embroider it. See *Design Your Own* below for details.

There is a complete size range for children and adults. Little ones will feel grown up with their own letter sweater.

DESIGN YOUR OWN

Letter Patterns—The illustration on page 73 shows a chart for duplicate-stitching an L. The L is shown in the exact size to be embroidered. You can design another letter. For instructions on duplicate-stitching, see page 20.

You Don't Have to be Varsity—If you like the pattern, knit it plain. Omit striping on the right sleeve and forget about the letter. Or stripe both sleeves!

SUITABLE YARN

Worsted-weight acrylic or wool yarn

YARN SHOWN

100% orlon-acrylic *Windrush* by Brunswick
3-1/2-ounce skeins = 100 grams
Main color: Maroon
Contrast color: Persimmon

TOOLS AND SUPPLIES

No. 4 and No. 8 needles or sizes to obtain correct gauge

STITCH PATTERNS

Stockinette Stitch—Alternate rows of knit and purl.
Varsity Ribbing—Repeat this pattern over two rows.
Row 1: Right-side. *Purl 2, knit 1, repeat from * to end of row.
Row 2: *Purl 1, knit 2; repeat from * to end of row.

GAUGE

With larger needles, in stockinette stitch:
4-1/2 stitches = 1 inch (2-1/2cm)
6 rows = 1 inch (2-1/2cm) approximately

Pattern continued on next page.

SIZE
Complete size range for children, women and men.

	CHILDREN			WOMEN			MEN		
	Small	Medium	Large	Small	Medium	Large	Small	Medium	Large
Body chest measurements	23-24 (59-61	26-28 66-71	30 76	30-31 76-79	32-34 82-87	36-38 92-97	38-40 97-102	42-44 107-112	46 inches 117cm)
Knitted chest measurements	26 (66	29 74	32 82	33 84	36 92	39 100	41 104	45 115	48 inches 122cm)
Width of knitted front and back	13 (33	14-1/2 37	16 40	16-1/2 42	18 46	19-1/2 50	20-1/2 52	22-1/2 57	24 inches 61cm)
Sleeve length—wrist to underarm	11 (28	13 33	15 38	17 43	18 46	18-1/2 47	19 48	19-1/2 50	21-1/2 inches 55cm)
Total length from beginning to shoulder	13-1/2 (34	15-1/2 39	17-1/2 44	21 54	22 56	23 59	24-1/2 62	26-1/2 67	28-1/2 inches 72cm)
Yarn required: Main color	2	3	3	4	4	4	5	6	6 skeins
Contrasting color	1	1	1	1	1	1	1	1	1 skein

Pattern
Check your gauge to avoid disappointment.

BACK With smaller needles, cast on	60	66	72	75	81	87	93	102	108 stitches
Work in varsity ribbing. Row 1: Purl 2, knit 1 across row. Row 2: Purl 1, knit 2 across row. Work this pattern for	3 (8	3-1/2 9	4 10	5 13	5-1/2 14	6 15	6-1/2 16	7-1/2 19	8-1/2 inches 21cm)
Change to larger needles and stockinette stitch. Work even until total length measures	13-1/2 (34	15-1/2 39	17-1/2 44	21 54	22 56	23 59	24-1/2 62	26-1/2 67	28-1/2 inches 72cm)
Bind off loosely in pattern.									
FRONT Work front same as back.									
LEFT SLEEVE With smaller needles, cast on	36	39	42	48	48	51	51	54	57 stitches
Work in varsity ribbing for End with row 2.	2 (5	2 5	2 5	3 8	3 8	3 8	3-1/2 9	3-1/2 9	3-1/2 inches 9cm)
Change to larger needles and stockinette stitch. Knit across first row and begin increases. Increase 1 stitch in first *and* last stitches, every inch (2-1/2cm) for total of	8 52	9 57	10 62	12 72	14 76	14 79	15 81	15 84	17 times 91 stitches

Pattern continued on next page.

Varsity-Letter Sweater	CHILDREN			WOMEN			MEN		
	Small	Medium	Large	Small	Medium	Large	Small	Medium	Large
Work even for total sleeve length of	11 (28	13 33	15 38	17 43	18 46	18-1/2 47	19 48	19-1/2 50	21-1/2 inches 55cm)
or desired length to underarm.									
Bind off loosely in pattern.									
RIGHT SLEEVE Work same as left sleeve for total length of	6 (15	7 18	8 20	9 22	9-1/2 24	10 25	10-1/2 27	11 28	12 inches 30cm)
or 1 inch (2-1/2cm) above elbow.									
Work varsity stripes in stockinette stitch. Beginning with knit row, work 6 rows in contrasting color, 4 rows in main color and 6 rows in contrasting color.									
At the same time, continue with increases. Work even in main color until right sleeve measures the same as left sleeve.									
Bind off loosely in pattern.									
FINISHING Join shoulder seams, leaving center neck opening of	7 (18	7 18	8 20	8-1/2 21	9 22	10 25	10 25	10-1/2 27	11 inches 28cm)
Mark armholes or side edges of main body with yarn loops. Total length of armholes with shoulder seam in middle.	11-1/2 (29	12-1/2 32	13-1/2 34	16 40	16-1/2 42	17-1/2 44	18 46	18-1/2 47	20 inches 51cm)
Sew in sleeves. Sew side and underarm seams. Form boat neckline by folding the neck edge under 1 inch (2-1/2cm) on front and back. Taper to nothing toward shoulders. Sew edge by catching only back of stitches on inside of sweater. Use matching thread color. Duplicate-stitch desired varsity letter with contrasting color yarn. Begin top of letter about 4 inches (10cm) below neckline on adult sizes, 2-1/2 inches (6cm) for children's sizes.									

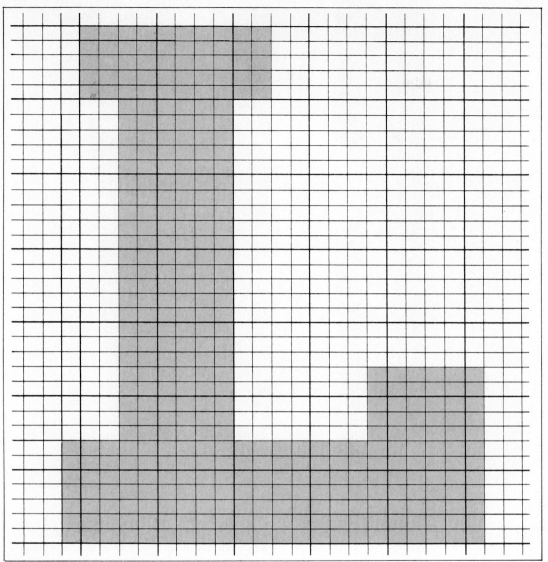

This chart is made on gauged graph paper.

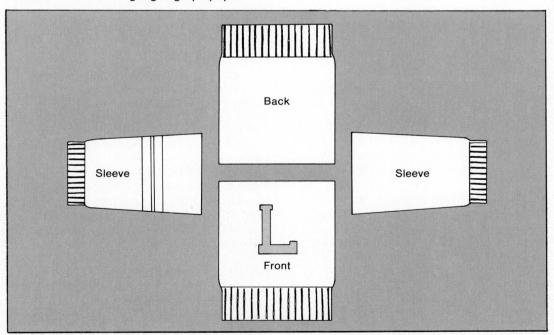

Pullover Vest, A-Line Skirt and Leg Warmers.

PULLOVER VEST

You'll wear this pullover vest for its good looks and extra warmth. Wear it as part of a three-piece outfit with the *A-Line Skirt,* page 77, and *Leg Warmers,* page 79. Wear it straight or belted, over a blouse or without a blouse. Add a scarf to make a smart, dressy outfit.

This is a simple pattern—seed-stitch borders frame the armholes and square neckline. Don't let the long instructions scare you. They spell out *exact* stitch counts for borders to save you counting.

DESIGN YOUR OWN
To Belt or Not to Belt—Knit a sling belt 1-1/4 inch (3cm) wide and 55 inches (140cm) long. With smaller needles, cast on seven stitches and work in seed-stitch pattern for desired length.
Make an Outfit—The *Leg Warmers,* page 79, and *A-Line Skirt,* page 77, create a versatile outfit for many occasions. Add a knitted *Star Hat,* page 32.
Hip-Length Tunic—For a slimming effect, lengthen the vest by adding 6 inches (15cm) to the straight stretch of stockinette stitch. You may have to cast on a few extra stitches at the beginning. For each 2 inches (5cm) that your hip measurements exceed your bust measurements, add five stitches to the back and five stitches to the front.

Between hip and waist decrease stitches every few rows until you have the number of stitches specified for the regular length. Don't forget to buy extra yarn.

SUITABLE YARN
Worsted-weight wool, acrylic or cotton yarn

YARN SHOWN
100% *Ragg Wool* by Columbia-Minerva
3-ounce hanks
Color: Oxford heather

TOOLS AND SUPPLIES
No. 6 and No. 8 needles or sizes to obtain correct gauge

STITCH PATTERNS
Ribbing—*Knit 1, purl 1, repeat from * across every row.
Stockinette Stitch—Alternate knit and purl rows.
Seed Stitch—Repeat this pattern over two rows.
    Row 1: *Knit 1, purl 1, repeat from * across row.
    Row 2: *Purl 1, knit 1, repeat from * across row.

GAUGE
With larger needles, in stockinette stitch:
5 stitches = 1 inch (2-1/2cm)
6 rows = 1 inch (2-1/2cm) approximately

SIZE
Women's small, medium and large.

	Small	**Medium**	**Large**
Body chest measurements	30-31 (76-79	32-34 82-87	36-38 inches 92-97cm)
Knitted chest measurements	32 (82	34 87	38 inches 97cm)
Width of knitted front and back	16 (40	17 43	19 inches 48cm)
Total length from beginning to shoulder	21 (54	21-1/2 55	22 inches 56cm)
Yarn required	2	2	3 hanks

Pattern

Check your gauge to avoid disappointment.

BACK

With smaller needles, cast on	72	76	86 stitches
Work in knit-1-purl-1 ribbing for	3 (8	3 8	3 inches 8cm)
Change to larger needles and stockinette stitch. Work even for total length of	12 (30	12 30	12 inches 30cm)
or 1-1/4 inches (3cm) less than desired length to underarm.			
End with right-side row. Begin seed-stitch border. On following 8 rows work in seed stitch on *first* and *last*	12	12	14 stitches
Work in stockinette stitch in between on	48	52	58 stitches
Shape armholes by binding off at beginning of next *two* rows	7	7	9 stitches
This reduces seed-stitch borders to for total stitch count of	5 52	5 62	5 stitches 68 stitches
Work even, work 5 stitches at both ends of needle in seed stitch for	6 (15	6-1/2 16	7 inches 18cm)
Begin working center in seed stitch as follows for	8	8	8 rows
Every row: in seed stitch in stockinette stitch in seed stitch in stockinette stitch in seed stitch	5 9 30 9 5	5 10 32 10 5	5 stitches 12 stitches 34 stitches 12 stitches 5 stitches
Bind off loosely in pattern.			

FRONT
Work front same as back until
3/4 inch (2cm) above armhole
bind offs.

Pattern continued on next page.

Helpful Hint

Some knitters cast on with a larger needle size than specified. This keeps edges from binding. When a pattern specifies size-5 needles for ribbing and size-7 needles for the main body, cast on with size-7 needles.

Pullover Vest	Small	Medium	Large
On next row work			
in seed stitch	5	5	5 stitches
in stockinette stitch	9	10	14 stitches
in seed stitch	30	32	34 stitches
in stockinette stitch	9	10	14 stitches
in seed stitch	5	5	5 stitches
Work even in established pattern for 8 rows. On next wrong-side row, divide for neckline.			
Work in seed stitch for	5	5	5 stitches
in stockinette stitch	9	10	14 stitches
in seed stitch	5	5	5 stitches
For right front, slip stitches just worked on holder	19	20	24 stitches
Bind off for center	20	22	24 stitches
Work left front in seed stitch	5	5	5 stitches
in stockinette stitch	9	10	14 stitches
in seed stitch	5	5	5 stitches
Work in established pattern over until total length equals back.	19	20	24 stitches
Bind off loosely in pattern.			
Work front right side to match front left side.			

FINISHING
Sew shoulder and side seams.

Helpful Hint

When you bind off, leave a 15- to 20-inch (38 to 51cm) tail for sewing seams. It saves time and is neat.

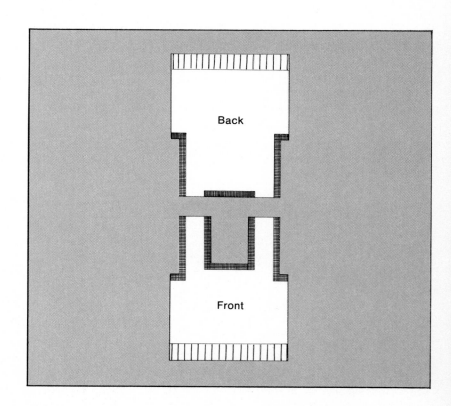

Back

Front

A-LINE SKIRT

The combination of classic style and contemporary tweedy look allows you to wear this skirt for years. Mix and match the skirt with the *Pullover Vest,* page 74, made from the same yarn, or with other pieces in your wardrobe. Add *Leg Warmers,* page 79, for a complete outfit. See photo on page 74.

Rotate the skirt from one wearing to the next to keep back from sitting out. A slip helps keep a smooth line.

DESIGN YOUR OWN

Two-Tone Outfits—Coordinate this skirt with knitted tops of the same or contrasting color. For a two-tone outfit, knit the top in a different color. Use the same yarn for the last rows of the skirt. Twelve rows equal a 2-inch (5cm) band. Ragg yarn comes in a brown-heather mixture that looks good with beige or brown. For a contrast in textures, knit a skirt in a smooth yarn with a mohair-type hem band. Add a top made from the same mohair-type yarn.

SUITABLE YARN

Worsted-weight wool or acrylic yarn

YARN SHOWN

100% wool *Ragg Wool* by Columbia-Minerva
3-ounce hanks
Color: Oxford heather

TOOLS AND SUPPLIES

No. 6 and No. 8 needles or sizes to obtain correct gauge
1 safety pin
1 yard (1m) 3/4-inch (2cm) elastic

STITCH PATTERNS

Ribbing—*Knit 1, purl 1; repeat from * across every row.
Seed Stitch—On an uneven number of stitches: *Knit 1, purl 1; repeat from * across, end row with knit 1.

GAUGE

With larger needles, in seed stitch:
4-1/2 stitches = 1 inch (2-1/2cm)
6 rows = 1 inch (2-1/2cm) approximately

SIZE

Women's small, medium and large.

	Small	Medium	Large
Body waist measurement	24-26 (61-66	27-28 69-71	29-32 inches 74-82cm)
Knitted waist measurement	27 (69	29 74	32 inches 82cm)
Knitted hip measurement	35 (89	39 100	42 inches 107cm)
Length of skirt	28 (71	29 74	29 inches 74cm)
Width at hemline	50 (127	54 138	58 inches 147cm)
Yarn required	4	5	6 hanks

Pattern

Check your gauge to avoid disappointment.

PANEL

Knit four panels alike.

	Small	Medium	Large
For waist, with smaller needles, cast on	28	32	36 stitches
Work in knit 1-purl-1 ribbing for 1 inch (2-1/2 cm). On final row of ribbing, increase 1 stitch for total of	29	33	37 stitches
Change to larger needles and seed stitch. Every row: *Knit 1, purl 1 repeat from * across, end with knit 1. While maintaining established seed-stitch pattern, increase 1 stitch at *both* ends of every 8th row 6 times for total of	41	45	47 stitches

Pattern continued on next page.

Helpful Hint

It's easy to turn regular yarn into brushed yarn or expensive-looking mohair. When you finish the garment or project, brush it with a stiff hairbrush.

Helpful Hints

Follow manufacturers' recommendations for washing knitted garments. Sturdy wool garments may be washed in a washing machine. Use cool water, unless otherwise recommended.

A-Line Skirt	Small	Medium	Large
Increase 1 stitch at *both* ends of every 12th row 8 times for total of	57	61	65 stitches
Work even until total length measures	29 (74	30 76	30 inches 76cm)
or 1 inch (2-1/2cm) more than desired length.			
Bind off loosely in pattern.			

FINISHING

Sew long sides of panels together with invisible-weaving method, page 16. Turn waist ribbing under 1 inch (2-1/2cm). Sew it to inside of skirt. Catch back of knitted stitches so sewing does not show on front. Leave opening in waistband to insert elastic.

Cut elastic to waist measurement, plus 3/4 inch (2cm). Attach safety pin to one end of elastic. Push pin and elastic through opening at waist. Guide both around inside waist. Overlap both ends of the elastic 3/4 inch (2cm), and sew together. Let elastic disappear inside waistband, then stitch opening closed.

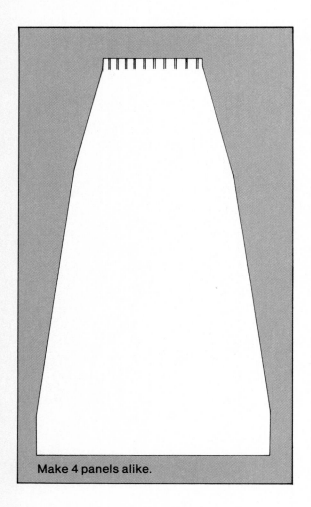

Make 4 panels alike.

LEG WARMERS

How can you keep leg warmers from sliding down your legs? Knit them in ribbing, which acts like elastic! The pattern is simple—it's a plain rectangle, sewn in a tube. Have fun using up yarn left from other projects. Knit leg warmers in colorful horizontal stripes. You will find specific directions below in *Design Your Own*.

DESIGN YOUR OWN
Show Your Knees—You may prefer calf warmers. They cover from the ankle to below the knee. Knit a total length of 14 inches (36cm) or to suit personal measurements.
Size Me—The width given will adjust to most people's legs. On skinny legs, warmers come up a little higher. They are shorter on heavier legs. For someone extra tall or extra short, add or subtract *rows*. For extra-heavy or extra-light legs, add or subtract *stitches*. In either case, check your gauge to arrive at the number to adjust.
Rib Me—Experiment with other ribbing combinations: knit 1, purl 1; or knit 4, purl 2. Cables running up the sides are another idea.
Color Me—Change color every few rows. If you use leftover yarn, try to obtain the same gauge by doubling thin yarns or work with smaller or larger needles. A few bulges created by uneven knitting add to the texture.

You may be more satisfied if you knit both leg warmers in the same stripe pattern. If this is your intention, save enough yarn of each color for the second tube.

SUITABLE YARN
Worsted-weight wool or acrylic yarn, particularly heavier, outdoor yarns

YARN SHOWN
100% *Ragg Wool* by Columbia-Minerva
3-ounce hanks
Color: Oxford heather

TOOLS AND SUPPLIES
No. 7 needles or size to obtain correct gauge

STITCH PATTERN
Ribbing—*Knit 2, purl 2; repeat from * across every row.

GAUGE
4-1/2 stitches = 1 inch (2-1/2cm), slightly stretched
6 rows = 1 inch (2-1/2cm) approximately

SIZE
One size fits average adults.

Approximate length	23 inches (59cm)
Knitted calf measurement	11-1/2 inches (29cm)
Yarn required	2 hanks

Pattern

Check your gauge to avoid disappointment.

Knit two tubes alike.

Loosely cast on	52 stitches
Work in ribbing for	23 inches (59cm)

or desired length.

Bind off loosely in pattern.

FINISHING
Sew center-back seam.

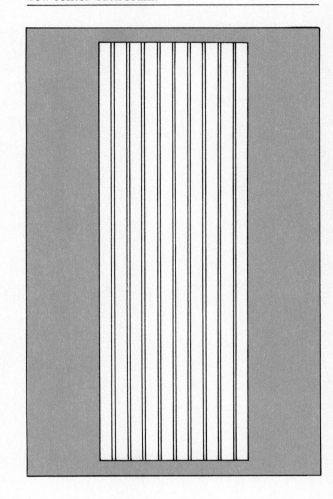

79

New Dazzlers

Special occasions call for new things. These dazzling sweaters are unusual and fun, and they'll give you a lift when you wear them.

When more than one size is given for a pattern, circle or highlight the column of the size you want to knit. This is described in *Learning to Knit,* page 7.

Hug-Me Stole.

HUG-ME

Like two loving arms, this unique garment will keep summer chills away or add romance to prom night. It's almost as good as a fur wrap. It can also double as a bedjacket.

The pattern is as simple as it is unusual. You knit one long rectangle, then sew ends together into cuffs. When it's finished, you have the comfort of a stole without having to constantly fumble to keep it in place. If you'd like a regular stole, you'll find instructions in *Design Your Own* below.

DESIGN YOUR OWN

Turn Me Over—The lace ribbing pattern looks attractive on both sides. Make the Hug-Me reversible by sewing flat seams. The purl side is preferred for the outside because edges roll over naturally, forming a soft collar.
Evening Stole—You can make a stole if you follow these instructions: With larger needles cast on 80 stitches. Knit in garter stitch—knit every row—for six rows. Change to lace ribbing, keeping the first and last 4 stitches of every row in garter stitch. Work even for 48 inches (122cm). Change to garter stitch for 6 rows. Bind off loosely in pattern.
Two Colors—For a change, make the stole in two colors. Knit garter stitches on all four borders in a color different from lace ribbing. For a good combination, use white for the lace and another color for borders.
Bedjacket—The Hug-Me makes a perfect bedjacket. Substitute a smoother yarn if you prefer a smoother finish.

SUITABLE YARN
Brushed or mohair yarns

YARN SHOWN
50% nylon-50% acrylic *Mirage* by Bucilla
1-3/4 ounces = 50 grams
Color: Peach

TOOLS AND SUPPLIES
No. 8 and No. 11 needles or sizes to obtain correct gauge

STITCH PATTERNS
Ribbing—*Knit 2, purl 2; repeat from * across every row.
Ribbed Lace—Repeat this pattern over two rows.
Row 1: Purl across row.
Row 2: *Knit 2, yarn over, knit 2 together; repeat from * across row, end with knit 2.

GAUGE
With larger needles, in lace pattern:
3 stitches = 1 inch (2-1/2cm) approximately
4 rows = 1 inch (2-1/2cm) approximately

SIZE

Total length	50 inches (128cm)
Yarn required	4 skeins

Pattern

Check your gauge to avoid disappointment.

With smaller needles, cast on	40 stitches
Work in knit-2-purl-2 ribbing for	6 inches (15cm)
On last row of ribbing, increase every stitch *except* first and last stitches for total of	1 stitch 78 stitches
Change to larger needles and lace pattern. Work even for	38 inches (97cm)
for total length of	44 inches (112cm)
On next right-side row, knit 2 stitches together across row, except last 2 stitches. This leaves	40 stitches
Change to smaller needles and knit-2-purl-2 ribbing pattern. Work even for	6 inches (15cm)
Bind off loosely in pattern.	

FINISHING
Sew edges of ribbing together to form cuffs. You can make cuffs longer by continuing seam for 4 inches (10cm) along lace pattern or as much as desired.

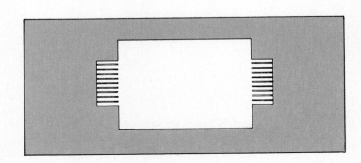

BLACK-AND-WHITE ZIGZAG

This lightly bloused sweater with puffed sleeves is knitted in two colors. Colors are divided with an unusual zigzag stitch. Black and white is always dramatic, but choose other color combinations for a softer look. Even in one color, you can create a contrast of textures. Work one side with a flat worsted yarn and the other with mohair or other fluffy yarn. *Design Your Own,* below, offers you more suggestions.

Half the number of stitches are cast on in one color and half are cast on in the other color. On every row, when you reach the color change, twist the two yarns around each other. This avoids gaps between the two colors.

Color patterns are knitted the same on the back and front, as well as the sleeves. This results in black-and-white sections alternating around the sweater.

DESIGN YOUR OWN

Color Combinations—Color choices are unlimited and depend on whether you like bold impact or a more subtle contrast. Bold combinations are red and black; turquoise and hot pink; yellow and orange. A combination of earth tones provides a mellow effect. Look for other ideas under *Color* in *Designing Your Own,* page 123.

Smoother Shoulders—For seaming shoulders together with the knitted method, page 16, you need four stitch holders. Instead of binding off all 66 (76) stitches on the back and front, knit 16 (19) stitches for the shoulder. Place them on a holder. Bind off 34 (40) stitches for the neck. Knit 16 (19) stitches for the shoulder, and place them on a holder. Knit shoulders together.

SUITABLE YARN

Worsted-weight cotton, acrylic or wool yarn

YARN SHOWN

100% cotton *Ecoss'Anny* by anny blatt
90 yards = 50 grams
Color A: White
Color B: Black

TOOLS AND SUPPLIES

No. 5 and No. 7 needles or sizes to obtain correct gauge
4 stitch holders, optional

STITCH PATTERNS

Ribbing—*Knit 2, purl 2; repeat from * across every row.
Stockinette Stitch—Alternating rows of knit and purl.
Zigzag Color Changes—As specified in the pattern.

GAUGE

With larger needles, in stockinette stitch:
5 stitches = 1 inch (2-1/2cm)
7 rows = 1 inch (2-1/2cm) approximately

SIZE

Women's small-medium and large.

	Small-Medium	Large
Body chest measurements	31-34 (79-87	36-38 inches 92-97cm)
Knitted chest measurements	35 (89	39 inches 100cm)
Width of knitted front and back	17-1/2 (44	19-1/2 inches 50cm)
Sleeve length to underarm	6 (15	6 inches 15cm)
Length from beginning to shoulder	20-1/2 (52	22 inches 56cm)
Yarn required Color A: White Color B: Black	4 4	5 skeins 5 skeins

Pattern

Check your gauge to avoid disappointment.

BACK

Change colors halfway across every row.
Twist yarns around each other each time you change colors.

With smaller needles, with white cast on	40	44 stitches
Continue casting on in black for total of	40 80	44 stitches 88 stitches
Work in knit-2-purl-2 ribbing for	2 (5	2 inches 5cm)

Pattern continued on next page.

Black-and-White Zigzag	Small-Medium	Large
Change to larger needles and stockinette stitch. Maintain color change. Increase evenly across first knit row	6	10 stitches
for total of	86	98 stitches
Establish zigzag pattern over 4 rows as follows: Carry yarn loosely across wrong-side as necessary.		
Row 1: Right-side. With white, knit	46	52 stitches
with black, knit	40	46 stitches
Row 2: Wrong-side. With black, purl	43	49 stitches
with white, purl	43	49 stitches
Row 3: With white, knit	40	46 stitches
with black, knit	46	52 stitches
Row 4: With black, purl	43	49 stitches
with white, purl	43	49 stitches
Continue to repeat these 4 rows for entire back.		
Begin armhole shaping when total length measures	13 (33	14 inches 36cm)
or desired length to underarm.		
At beginning of next 2 rows, bind off	5	5 stitches
At beginning *and* end of following knit rows, decrease 1 stitch	5	5 times
This leaves	66	78 stitches
Work even until armhole measures	7-1/2 (19	8 inches 20cm)
Bind off all stitches on following knit row.		
FRONT Work front same as back.		
SLEEVES With smaller needles, with white cast on	26	32 stitches
Continue casting on in black	26	32 stitches
for total of	52	64 stitches
Change colors halfway across rows. Work in knit-2-purl-2 ribbing for	1-1/4 (3	1-1/4 inches 3cm)
Change to larger needles and stockinette stitch. Increase evenly across first row	16	16 stitches
for total of	68	80 stitches
Establish zigzag pattern over 4 rows as follows: Row 1: Right-side. With white, knit	37	43 stitches
with black, knit	31	37 stitches
Row 2: Wrong-side. With black, purl	34	40 stitches
with white, purl	34	40 stitches
Row 3: With white, knit	31	37 stitches
with black, knit	37	43 stitches
Row 4: With black, purl	34	40 stitches
with white, purl	34	40 stitches

Pattern continued on next page.

Black-and-White Zigzag	Small-Medium	Large
Repeat these 4 rows until total length of sleeve measures	6 (15	6 inches 15cm)
or desired length to underarm.		
Continue to maintain established color changes. Begin armhole shaping. At beginning of next 2 rows, bind off	5	5 stitches
At beginning *and* end of following knit rows, decrease	1 5	1 stitch 5 times
This leaves	48	60 stitches
Work even until armhole measures	6 (15	6-1/2 inches 16cm)
Form soft, puffy cap on following purl row. Purl 2 stitches together across entire row. This leaves	24	30 stitches
On following knit row, knit 2 stitches together across row.		
On next row, bind off all remaining stitches.		

FINISHING
Join shoulder seams for 3-1/2 inches (9cm). Set in sleeves. Sew side and sleeve seams. Form boat neckline by folding under 1 inch (2-1/2cm) at midpoint on front and back. Taper to nothing toward shoulders. Tack down by catching only the back of stitches on the inside of sweater. Use same thread colors.

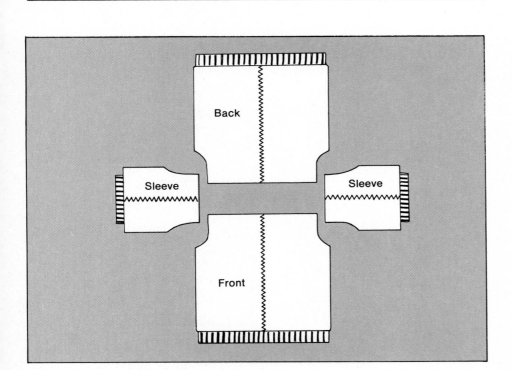

Back

Sleeve

Sleeve

Front

Butterfly Jacket.

BUTTERFLY JACKET

Whether a conservative dresser or a fashion sophisticate, this comfortable jacket is great for your wardrobe. It is knitted in white, which goes with everything. The unusual style accentuates the depth of the ribbing and brings out sculptural lines.

Once you understand the construction of the three basic pieces, it's easy to follow directions. The back is worked in knit-2-purl-2 ribbing to the armholes. Stitches are added at the sides for sleeves.

For each front piece, stitches are cast on for sides and sleeves. The sleeve section is worked in knit-2-purl-2 ribbing. Ribbing on the front section increases as you go along to create a fan effect.

To accommodate the large number of stitches, a circular needle is recommended. Knit back and forth as you would on a regular pair of needles.

Everything will become clear when you start knitting. See the diagram on page 89. Knitters say this is not a difficult pattern to work, and they enjoy its rhythm.

DESIGN YOUR OWN

Larger Size—There is a lot of give to this jacket, but you can increase the size, if necessary. For each extra inch (2-1/2cm) desired, add an extra knit-2-purl-2 rib, a total of 4 stitches. Add this at the wrist end of sleeves and across the back width. Fronts remain the same.

Longer Sleeves—Sleeves can be lengthened by blocking. Do *not* block the back and fronts. Pin sleeves at the shoulder line, pull longer, then block.

SUITABLE YARN

Heavy-weight worsted wool or acrylic yarn
To maintain jacket shape, yarn should have a hard finish, such as *Icelandic* yarns.

YARN SHOWN

100% wool *Nordland* by Joseph Galler
110 yards = 100 grams
Color: Natural white

TOOLS AND SUPPLIES

No. 10 circular needle or size to obtain correct gauge
1 stitch holder
2 ring markers

STITCH PATTERN

Ribbing—*Knit 2, purl 2; repeat from * across every row. Increases on the front are indicated.

GAUGE

On slightly stretched ribbing:
3-1/2 stitches = 1 inch (2-1/2cm)

SIZE

One size fits most women.

Yarn required	10 skeins

Pattern
Check your gauge to avoid disappointment.

BACK

Cast on	54 stitches
Knitting back and forth on circular needle, work in knit-2-purl-2 ribbing for	54 rows
At the end of next 2 rows, increase for sleeves by casting on for total of	56 stitches 166 stitches
Work in established ribbing for	18 rows
Begin shaping sleeves and shoulders. Bind off on both sides	4 stitches 10 times
This leaves	86 stitches
Bind off on both sides	3 stitches 2 times
This leaves	74 stitches
Bind off on both sides	4 stitches 1 time
This leaves	66 stitches
Bind off on both sides	10 stitches 1 time
This leaves	46 stitches
Bind off on both sides	7 stitches 2 times
This leaves	18 stitches
Place on holder remaining	18 stitches

RIGHT FRONT

Odd rows start on sleeves.
Even rows start on front.

Cast on	93 stitches
Row 1: In knit-1-purl-2 ribbing, work over Place ring marker on needle.	39 stitches
Work in knit-2-purl-2 ribbing over Carry marker up every row to indicate division between front and sleeve	54 stitches
Row 2: Continue purl-2-knit-2 ribbing over	54 sleeve stitches
Work purl-1-knit-2 ribbing over	39 sleeve stitches
Rows 3 and 4: Work in established ribbing.	
Row 4: Increase 1 stitch in each knit stitch up to marker, making	52 front stitches
Continue in established knit-2-purl-2 ribbing on remaining	54 front stitches
Rows 6 through 14: Work in established ribbing over	106 stitches
Row 15: Before reaching marker, increase 1 stitch in each of first knit stitch, making	65 front stitches

Pattern continued on next page.

Helpful Hint

Make knitteds dressy by knitting thin metallic yarn along with regular yarn.

Butterfly Jacket

Work in established knit-2-purl-2 ribbing over	54 sleeve stitches
for total of	119 stitches
Rows 16 through 19: Work in established knit-3-purl-2 ribbing over	65 front stitches
Work in knit-2-purl-2 ribbing over	54 sleeve stitches
Row 20: Begin binding off for sleeves. At beginning of row, bind off	4 stitches
Continue in established ribbing pattern across row.	
Row 21: Work in established ribbing pattern over	115 stitches
Row 22: At beginning of row, bind off Continue in established ribbing patterns.	4 stitches
Row 23: Work in established ribbing pattern over	111 stitches
Row 24: At beginning of row, bind off Continue in established ribbing patterns.	4 stitches
Row 25: Before reaching marker, increase 1 stitch in each first knit stitch, making	78 front stitches
Work in established ribbing pattern over	42 sleeve stitches
for total of	120 stitches
Row 26: At beginning of row, bind off	4 stitches
Work in knit-2-purl-2 ribbing up to marker. Work in knit-4-purl-2 ribbing as established.	
Row 27: Work in established knit-4-purl-2 ribbing over	78 front stitches
Work in knit-2-purl-2 ribbing for	38 sleeve stitches
Rows 28, 30, 32 and 34: Work as row 26. Bind off at the beginning of each row	4 stitches
Rows 29, 31, 33: Work as row 27.	
Row 35: Before reaching marker, increase 1 stitch in each of first knit stitches for total of	91 front stitches
Continue in established ribbing across	22 sleeve stitches
Row 36: At beginning of row, bind off	4 stitches
Work in knit-2-purl-2 ribbing to marker. Work in knit-5-purl 2 ribbing over remaining	91 stitches
Row 37: Work in established ribbing over	91 front stitches 18 sleeve stitches
for total of	109 stitches
Row 38: At beginning of row, bind off	4 stitches
Work in knit-2-purl-2 ribbing to marker. Work in knit-5-purl-2 ribbing over remaining	91 front stitches
Row 39: Work in established ribbing pattern over	91 front stitches 14 sleeve stitches

Pattern continued on next page.

Butterfly Jacket

for total of	105 stitches
Row 40: At beginning of row, bind off Continue across row in established ribbing patterns.	3 stitches
Row 41: Work in established ribbing patterns over	91 front stitches 11 sleeve stitches
for total of	102 stitches
Row 42: At beginning of row, bind off	3 stitches
Continue across row in established ribbing pattern.	
Row 43: Work in established ribbing pattern over	91 front stitches 8 sleeve stitches
for total of	99 stitches
Row 44: At beginning of row, bind off	4 stitches
Continue across row in established ribbing pattern	91 front stitches 4 sleeve stitches
for total of	95 stitches
Row 45: Before marker, increase 1 stitch in each of first knit stitches of knit-5-purl-2 ribbing, making	104 front stitches
Continue in established knit-2-purl-2 ribbing across row over	4 sleeve stitches
Row 46: At beginning of row, bind off	4 sleeve stitches
Continue across row in established ribbing pattern over	104 stitches
Rows 47 and 48: Work in established ribbing pattern over	104 front stitches
Row 49: Increase 1 stitch in each of first knit stitches of knit-6 ribbing	6 times
Increase 1 stitch in each of first and last stitches of knit-6 ribbing	7 times
for total of	124 front stitches
Rows 50 through 54: Work in established ribbing patterns of 7 + 2 and 8 + 2.	
Row 55: Combine front and back by picking up 9 stitches of 18 back-neck stitches.	
Rows 56 through 58: Work in established ribbing pattern over	133 stitches
Bind off all stitches in ribbing.	

LEFT FRONT
Work left front same as right front, but
reverse shaping.

FINISHING
Pin front and back of sleeves together at
shoulders and underarms. Weave seams
together. Sew side seams.

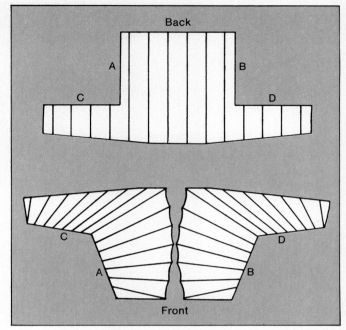

Red, White and Blue Sweater.

RED, WHITE AND BLUE

The traditional sailor's middy is adapted here to a comfortable, stylish, oversize shirt. It's a new look to an old favorite.

The pattern is made in one size only. The sweater fits women with bust measurements between 31 and 36 inches (79 and 92cm).

This garment is worked in stockinette stitch, with a hem of reverse-stockinette stitch. The plain sleeve is worked as part of the back and front. Shoulders are joined with the knitting-together method for a smooth seam. See page 16.

In this asymmetrical design, the left sleeve is white. It is knitted as part of the back and front. The right sleeve is striped. Stitches are picked up at the sides of the main body pieces.

The red tie is knitted with embroidery yarn. Embroidery yarn comes in smaller hanks than knitting yarn.

DESIGN YOUR OWN
Year-Round Comfort—A middy is ideal for summer, by itself or layered. For cooler weather, select other colors, and change from cotton to orlon or wool yarn.
Tie-Knotting Trouble—You may not know how to tie a traditional knot on the tie. Ask someone to tie the knot for you. When you have a satisfactory knot, don't untie it. Slip the long loop off and on over your head.
Symmetry Shirt—Want two striped sleeves or two plain ones? Reverse one side of the main body pieces to match the other side. It's easy to become a designer.
Navy Type?—Add brass buttons to the shoulder of the striped sleeve.

SUITABLE YARN
Worsted-weight cotton, acrylic or wool yarn

YARN SHOWN
For sweater:
100% cotton *Ecoss'Anny* by anny blatt
90 yards = 50 grams
Main color: White
Stripe color: Royal blue
For tie:
Red Parisian-cotton embroidery yarn

TOOLS AND SUPPLIES
For sweater:
No. 7 needles or size to obtain correct gauge
4 stitch holders
For tie:
No. 4 needles or size to obtain correct gauge

STITCH PATTERNS
Stockinette Stitch—Alternating rows of knit and purl.
Reverse-Stockinette Stitch—Same as stockinette stitch, but grainy texture is used as the right-side.

GAUGE
For sweater:
5 stitches = 1 inch (2-1/2cm)
6 rows = 1 inch (2-1/2cm) approximately
For tie:
8 stitches = 1 inch (2-1/2cm)

SIZE
One size fits bust measurements between 31 and 36 inches (79 and 92cm).

Body chest measurements	31-36 inches (79-92cm)
Knitted chest measurements	39 inches (100cm)
Width of knitted front and back	19-1/2 inches (50cm)
Sleeve length to underarm	6 inches (15cm)
Length from beginning to shoulder	22 inches (56cm)
Yarn required	
White	10 skeins
Royal	1 skein
Red embroidery thread	4 hanks

Pattern

Check your gauge to avoid disappointment.

FRONT

With larger needles and white, cast on	100 stitches
Beginning with knit row, work in reverse-stockinette stitch for	6 rows
Purl across 7th row. This makes 2 rows of purling for hem.	
Work in stockinette stitch for	13 inches (33cm)
measured from hem ridge or desired length to underarm.	
At end of next right-side row, cast on for left sleeve for total of	33 stitches 133 stitches
At beginning of next wrong-side row, bind off for right underarm	15 stitches
Work even on remaining until sleeve depth is	118 stitches 9 inches (22cm)
On next right-side row, knit for shoulder	58 stitches
Bind off for center	50 stitches
Knit for other shoulder	10 stitches
Place shoulder stitches on two holders. For right shoulder For left shoulder	10 stitches 58 stitches

BACK
Work back same as front. Reverse sleeve and underarm shaping.

SEAMING
Using knitting-together method, join 10 stitches of back and front of right shoulder. Join back and front of left shoulder, 58 stitches wide.

Pattern continued in next column.

RIGHT SLEEVE
Right sleeve has 9 stripes. Each stripe is 6 rows wide. Stripes alternate in royal blue and white, plus a royal-blue hem.

With right-side facing you, with royal blue pick up at right armhole edge	90 stitches
Work in stockinette stitch	6 rows

Change color every 6 rows for a total of 5 royal-blue stripes and 4 white stripes. Begin hem by continuing with royal blue. Work 2 rows of purling. Work in reverse-stockinette stitch for 3 rows.

Bind off loosely in pattern.

FINISHING
Sew side seams. Turn right sleeve under at hem ridge and hem. Hem left sleeve by folding under last 3 rows. Form boat neckline by folding under midpoint on front and back about 1 inch (2-1/2cm). Taper to nothing toward shoulders, then tack down. Catch only back of stitches on inside of sweater. Hem bottom of sweater.

TIE
Work 2 strands of red embroidery yarn.

Cast on	16 stitches
Work in knit-1-purl-1 ribbing for	60 inches (152cm)

Bind off loosely in pattern.

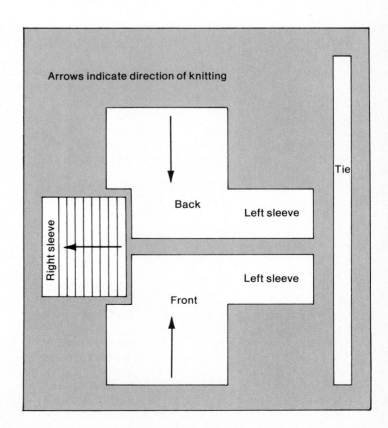

Arrows indicate direction of knitting

SWEATER COAT

You can knit this sweater coat in the time it usually takes to make a sweater if you use bulky yarn. The coat shown here is a block knit. Wear it hanging straight from the shoulders, or wrap it and tie it with a belt. For more versatility, tie the belt as a scarf and make the hood into a totebag.

DESIGN YOUR OWN
Edging—With dark color, crochet around front and neck edges.
Button Up—Attach a button 1-1/2 inches (4cm) below the left neck edge. Crochet a buttonhole loop at the right edge.
Totebag—Make a totebag. Follow instructions for knitting the hood, then sew the side seam. If desired, line the bag with fabric cut the same size as the original knitted rectangle. Knit a strap in garter stitch, using the dark yarn. Make the strap six stitches wide and 40 inches (1m) long. To prevent stretching, line the strap with a piece of webbing in a compatible color.

SUITABLE YARN
Bulky acrylic or wool yarn

YARNS SHOWN
60% acrylic-40% nylon *Big Berella Bulky* by Bernat
3-1/2 ounces = 100 grams
Colors: Copper heather and Carmel heather

TOOLS AND SUPPLIES
No. 11 needles or size to obtain correct gauge

STITCH PATTERNS
Garter Stitch—Knit every row.
Brick-and-Mortar Stitch—Repeat this pattern over eight rows.
Rows 1 and 2: With light color, knit across row.
Row 3: With dark color, knit 1, *slip 1 as if to knit with yarn in back, knit 3; repeat from * across row, end with slip 1, knit 1.
Row 4: With dark color, purl 1, *slip 1 as if to purl with yarn in front, purl 3; repeat from * across row, end with slip 1, purl 1.
Rows 5 and 6: With light color, knit across row.
Row 7: With dark color, knit 3, *slip 1 with yarn in back, knit 3; repeat from * across row.
Row 8: With dark color, purl 3, *slip 1, with yarn in front, purl 3; repeat from * across row.

GAUGE
3 stitches = 1 inch (2-1/2cm)
4 rows = 1 inch (2-1/2cm) approximately

SIZE
One size fits most women.

Knitted chest measurements	45 inches (115cm)
Width of knitted back	22 inches (56cm)

Width of knitted front	11-1/2 inches (29cm)
Sleeve length	16 inches (40cm)
Length from beginning to shoulder	31 inches (79cm)
Yarn required, including hood and belt: Light color Dark color	6 skeins 7 skeins

Pattern
Check your gauge to avoid disappointment.

BACK

With dark color, cast on	66 stitches
Work in garter stitch for	4 inches (10cm)
Change to brick pattern. Work even until total length measures or desired length to shoulder.	31 inches (79cm)
End with row 4 or 8 of brick pattern.	
Bind off loosely with light color.	

FRONTS
Work two fronts alike.

With dark color, cast on	35 stitches
Work in garter stitch for	4 inches (10cm)

Change to brick pattern. Work even until length measures same as back. End with row 4 or 8 of brick pattern. Bind off loosely with light color.

SLEEVES
Work two sleeves alike.

With dark color, cast on	54 stitches
Work in garter stitch for	4 inches (10cm)
Change to brick pattern. Work even until total length measures or desired length to underarm.	16 inches (40cm)
End with row 4 or 8 of brick pattern.	
Bind off loosely with light color.	

HOOD
Hood is optional.

With dark color, cast on	71 stitches
Work in garter stitch for	6 rows
Change to brick pattern. Work even for total length of	10 inches (25cm)

End with row 4 or 8 of brick pattern. Bind off loosely with light color.

Pattern continued on next page.

Helpful Hint

You can stretch a sweater if it's too tight. Dampen it, pull it wider or longer, and let it dry on a towel.

Sweater Coat

BELT

Belt is optional.

With dark color, cast on	6 stitches
Work in garter stitch for	60 inches (152cm)

or desired length.

Bind off loosely in pattern.

FINISHING

For sewing, make knitting yarn thinner by discarding one strand. Beginning at arm edges, sew shoulder seams for 8 inches (20cm). Sew sleeves to back and fronts. Sew underarm and side seams. Leave bottom of side seams open for 3 inches (7cm) for side slits. Fold hood in half along short edge, and seam longer back edge. Sew hood to neck edge of coat.

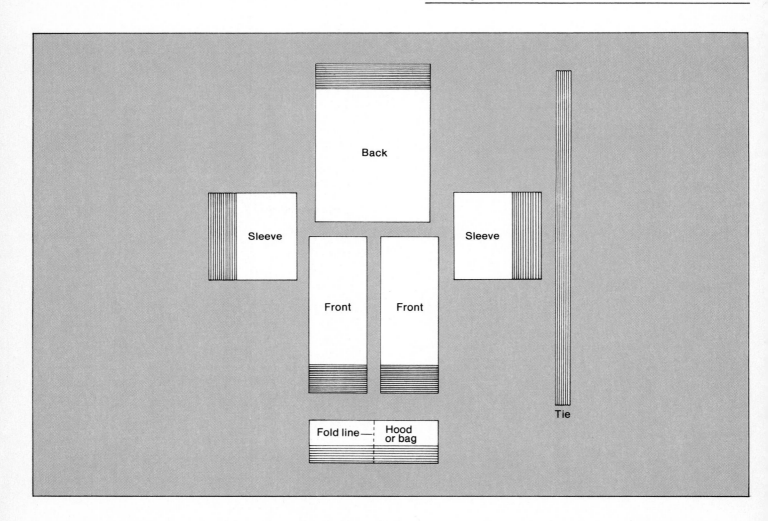

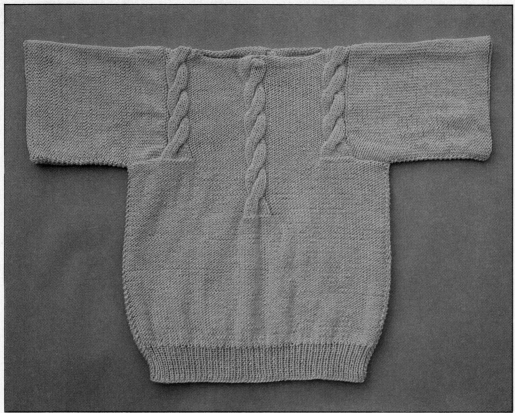

Tri-Cable Sweater.

TRI-CABLE

Cables form one of the most attractive stitch patterns. On this sweater, the front and back are knitted in one piece to give an uninterrupted flow of side cables. Work on the front is continued directly over the shoulders, into the back, creating a one-row opening for the neck.

DESIGN YOUR OWN

Extra-Long—If you like the sweater belted, make it longer on the front and back between waist ribbing and cables. This is done as you knit in reverse-stockinette stitch.

Knitted-On Sleeves—Instead of knitting sleeves separately, create smooth armhole seams by knitting sleeves directly into the armholes. With the right-side of the front-back piece facing you, with larger needles pick up 80 stitches along the cabled armhole edges. Knit even in reverse-stockinette stitch for 10 inches (25cm). Begin stockinette-stitch hem by knitting two purl rows in succession. Work even for 1 inch (2-1/2cm), then bind off.

Double Color, Triple Cable—Knit cables in a different color from the main body.

SUITABLE YARN

Worsted-weight cotton, acrylic or wool yarn

YARN SHOWN

100% cotton *Ecoss'Anny* by anny blatt
90 yards = 50 grams
Color: Mint green

TOOLS AND SUPPLIES

No. 5 and No. 7 needles or sizes to obtain correct gauge
1 cable needle

STITCH PATTERNS

Ribbing—*Knit 1, purl 1; repeat from * across every row.
Reverse-Stockinette Stitch—Repeat this pattern over two rows.
    Row 1: Knit across row.
    Row 2: Purl across row.
Cable Stitch—Repeat this pattern over 10 stitches and 12 rows.
    Rows 1, 3 and 5: Knit 10 stitches.
    Rows 2, 4 and 6: Purl 10 stitches.
    Row 7: Slip 5 stitches on a cable needle and hold at back of work. Knit 5 stitches from left needle. Knit 5 stitches from the cable needle.
    Rows 8, 10 and 12: Purl all 10 stitches.
    Rows 9 and 11: Knit all 10 stitches.
A complete cable is 12 rows, with the twist occuring in the middle.
Stockinette Stitch—Repeat this pattern over two rows for sleeve hems.
    Row 1: Purl across row.
    Row 2: Knit across row.

GAUGE

Reverse-stockinette stitch, with larger needles:
5 stitches = 1 inch (2-1/2cm)
8 rows = 1 inch (2-1/2cm) approximately

Helpful Hint

Save your gauge swatches, and sew them together into a scarf or patchwork pillow.

SIZE
Women's small and medium.

	Small	Medium
Body chest measurements	30-32 (76-82	33-34 inches 84-87cm)
Knitted chest measurements	34 (87	36 inches 92cm)
Width of knitted front and back	17 (43	18 inches 46cm)
Sleeve length	7-1/2 (19	7-1/2 inches 19cm)
Total length from beginning to shoulder	21 (54	21 inches 54cm)
Yarn required	10	11 skeins

Pattern

Check your gauge to avoid disappointment.

	Small	Medium
ONE-PIECE FRONT AND BACK With smaller needles, cast on for front waist.	80	84 stitches
Work in knit-1-purl-1 ribbing for	2 (5	2 inches 5cm)
Change to larger needles and reverse-stockinette stitch. Begin with purl row and increase evenly spaced across for total of	6 86	6 stitches 90 stitches
Work even until total length measures	11 (28	11 inches 28cm)
Establish center cable on next purl row: Purl	38	40 stitches
knit for center cable	10	10 stitches
purl	38	40 stitches
Work in established reverse-stockinette and cable pattern for two complete cables for total of	24	24 rows
Twists take place in rows 7 and 14. At same time, on rows 23 and 24, last two rows of second cable, decrease for underarm at beginning of both rows.	8	8 stitches
This leaves	70	74 stitches
Row 25: Establish side cable as follows: Purl	2	2 stitches
knit for side cable	10	10 stitches
purl	18	20 stitches
knit for center cable	10	10 stitches
purl	18	20 stitches
knit for side cable	10	10 stitches
purl	2	2 stitches
Work even in newly established patterns of reverse-stockinette and cables until armhole measures about	8 (20	8 inches 20cm)

Pattern continued on next page.

Tri-Cable	Small	Medium
Divide for neckline on first row *beginning* fifth side cable sequence. This is a right-side row.		
Work in pattern across	15	17 stitches
Bind off	40	40 stitches
Work in pattern across	15	17 stitches
On next row, work in pattern across	15	17 stitches
Cast on for neck	40	40 stitches
Work in pattern for	15	17 stitches

Work back to match front for total of 8 side cables—4 cables on front and 4 cables on back. Work 6 center cables after neckline. Be sure twists occur on same row for all three cables.

SLEEVES
Make two sleeves alike.

	Small	Medium
With larger needles, cast on	80	80 stitches
Work in stockinette stitch for hem for	1 (2-1/2	1 inch 2-1/2cm)
Change to reverse-stockinette stitch by working two purl rows in succession. Work even for	10 (25	10 inches 25cm)

Bind off loosely in pattern.

FINISHING
For smoother seams, separate one strand of knitting yarn for sewing. Sew top of sleeves to cabled armhole edges. Sew about 1-1/2 inches (4cm) of the *underarm edges* of sleeves to underarm bind off of front and back. See illustration. *Corners of sleeves fit into corners created on main body.* Sew side and underarm seams. Fold neckline edges under 3/4 inch (2cm) at center. Taper to nothing toward shoulders. Stitch invisibly by catching only back of the knitted stitches. Turn under sleeve hems, and stitch down invisibly.

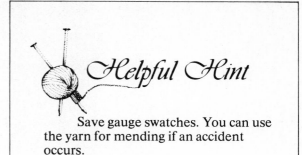

Helpful Hint

Save gauge swatches. You can use the yarn for mending if an accident occurs.

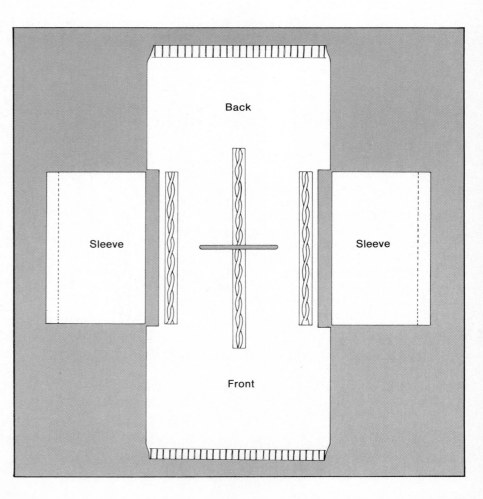

Daisy-Petals Ensemble.

DAISY-PETALS ENSEMBLE

Versatility and elegance mark this cardigan-and-camisole set. You'll enjoy wearing the cardigan and camisole together or separately. It's great for wearing at home or when traveling.

This ensemble is knitted in stockinette stitch, but yarn changes and making loops keep you from being bored. You should have some knitting experience before you tackle the cardigan. Take one row at a time and you'll do fine.

The cardigan hangs open and the camisole has an elastic top. The medium size fits both slightly smaller or slightly larger bust measurements than usual. *Design Your Own,* below, offers more sizing suggestions.

DESIGN YOUR OWN
Simplified Version—Instead of three colors, use one color.
Other Colors—Going out for the evening? Make a dressy sweater set by knitting with gold metallic thread. Use it double for color C. Another color suggestion might be lavender, lilac and burgundy.
Pullover—Change the cardigan pattern into a boatneck pullover to wear any time. Knit two backs. Sew shoulders together for 4-1/2 inches (12cm), leaving a center-neck opening. Turn neck edges under about 3/4 inch (2cm), tapering to nothing at the shoulders.
Smoother Shoulders—For seaming shoulders together with the knitted method shown on page 16, divide the 40 stitches on the back. Work 10 stitches, for the right shoulder, 20 stitches for the neck and 10 stitches for the left shoulder.
Other Sizes—The size shown is versatile. You can make the garment smaller by using smaller needles. To make a larger garment, use larger needles. The fuzziness of mohair yarn lends itself well to a tighter or looser knit.

Measure the gauge on your test swatch. Calculate it in the required chest measurement.

SUITABLE YARN
For cardigan:
　　Color A: Wool or acrylic-mohair yarn
　　Colors B and C: Shiny cotton, linen or synthetic sport-weight yarn used double, or worsted-weight yarn used single
For camisole:
　　Shiny cotton, linen or synthetic sport-weight yarn, in two colors used double, or worsted-weight yarn used single

YARN SHOWN

For cardigan:

    Color A: 100% wool *Majestic Mohair* by Joseph Galler
    70 yards = 40 grams
    Color: White
    Color B: Cotton-and-linen *Lino Fino* by Joseph Galler
    170 yards = 50 grams
    Color: Wheat
    Color C: Cotton-and-linen *Lino Fino* by Joseph Galler
    170 yards = 50 grams
    Color: Cream

For camisole:

    Color B: Cotton-and-linen *Lino Fino* by Joseph Galler
    170 yards = 50 grams
    Color: Wheat
    Color C: Cotton-and-linen *Lino Fino* by Joseph Galler
    170 yards = 50 grams
    Color: Cream

TOOLS AND SUPPLIES

For cardigan:

    No. 8 and No. 11 needles or sizes to obtain correct gauge
    2 stitch holders

For camisole:

    No. 5 and No. 8 needles or sizes to obtain correct gauge
    1 yard (1m) 1/8-inch-wide (3mm) elastic

STITCH PATTERNS

For cardigan and camisole:

Ribbing—*Knit 1, purl 1; repeat from * across every row.
Giant-Daisy Stitch—Six rows of stockinette stitch followed by two patterned rows. Instructions contain details, but you can find additional information about making daisy petals in *Sampler of Stitches,* page 29.
Color sequence for cardigan:

    Rows 1 to 6: Color A, shown in white mohair
    Rows 7 to 10: Color B, shown in wheat *Lino Fino,* used double
    Rows 11 to 12: Color C, shown in cream *Lino Fino,* used double
    Rows 13 to 16: Color A, shown in white mohair

For camisole only:

Stockinette Stitch—Alternate knit and purl rows.
Reverse-Stockinette Stitch—This stitch is used for the hem. Alternate rows of knit and purl.

GAUGE

For cardigan:

    With larger needles, in daisy-petal stitch:
    3 stitches = 1 inch (2-1/2cm)
    4 rows = 1 inch (2-1/2cm) approximately

For camisole:

    With larger needles, in stockinette stitch:
    4 stitches = 1 inch (2-1/2cm)
    5 rows = 1 inch (2-1/2cm) approximately

Helpful Hint

Rest your hands once in awhile and stretch them. This is especially helpful if you're a tight knitter.

SIZE

Women's small-medium
for cardigan and camisole.

Body chest measurement	32-34 inches (82-87cm)
Knitted chest measurement	36 inches (92cm)
Width of knitted front and back	18 inches (46cm)
Cardigan sleeve length to underarm	10-1/2 inches (27cm)
Length of cardigan, from beginning to shoulder	20 inches (51cm)
Length of camisole to underarm	12 inches (30cm)

Yarn required
For cardigan:

Color A	5 skeins
Color B	3 skeins
Color C	1 skein

For camisole:

Color C	2 skeins
Color B	1 skein

If you are knitting the cardigan and camisole, one ball of color C is enough for both.

Pattern continued on next page.

Helpful Hint

For sewing seams and working in bulky yarn ends, use needles with very large eyes—even larger than tapestry needles.

Cardigan Pattern

Check your gauge to avoid disappointment.

BACK

With smaller needles and color A, cast on	54 stitches
Work in knit-1-purl-1 ribbing for	2 inches (5cm)

Change to larger needles. Work 8 rows in daisy-petals-stitch pattern and 16-row color sequence at the same time. See page 29 for instructions on working the daisy-petal stitch.

Continue with color A.
Rows 1, 3 and 5: Knit across row.
Rows 2, 4 and 6: Purl across row.
Change to color B. Use yarn double.
Row 7: Knit 4 *knit 1, loop, knit 2, loop, knit 2, loop, knit 5; repeat from * across.
Row 8: *Purl 5, purl 2 together, purl 1, purl 2 together, purl 1, purl 2 together; repeat from * across. End row with purl 4.
Row 9: Knit across row.
Row 10: Purl across row.
Change to color C. Use yarn double.

Row 11: Knit across row.
Row 12: Purl across row.
Change to color A.
Rows 13 and 15: Knit across row.
Rows 14 and 16: Purl across row.
Repeat this 16-row sequence for entire cardigan.

Work even for a total length of	13 inches (33cm)

or desired length to underarm.

Begin shaping armhole. At beginning of next 2 rows, bind off	4 stitches
At beginning *and* end of next 3 knit rows, decrease	1 stitch
This leaves	40 stitches
Work even until armhole measures	7 inches (18cm)
On following knit row, bind off all	40 stitches

If this is row 7 in the pattern sequence, do *not* make any daisy loops.

LEFT FRONT

With smaller needles and color A, cast on	32 stitches
Work in knit-1-purl-1 ribbing for	2 inches (5cm)

Change to larger needles. Work 16-row sequence, beginning with color A. Row 1: Knit	27 stitches
For center bands to be worked later, place on holder	5 stitches

Pattern continued on next page.

Cardigan Pattern

Rows 2, 4 and 6: Purl across row.
Rows 3 and 5: Knit across row.
Change to color B.
Row 7: Knit 7 *knit 1, loop, knit 2, loop,
knit 2, loop, knit 5; repeat from * twice.
Row 8: *Purl 5, purl 2 together, purl 1,
purl 2 together, purl 1, purl 2 together;
repeat from * twice, end with purl 7.
Rows 9 through 16: Work in sequence
to match back.

Begin center-neck shaping when total length measures	8 inches (20cm)
Decrease 1 stitch at neck edge every by knitting to last 3 stitches.	4th row
Knit 2 together, knit 1	10 times
When total length measures	13 inches (33cm)
or same length to armhole as back, begin armhole shaping.	
At same time, continue neckline shaping. At beginning of the next knit row, bind off	4 stitches
Bind off on same sequence row to match back. At beginning of following 3 knit rows, decrease 1 stitch until you have only	10 stitches
Work even until armhole measures	7 inches (18cm)
or same length as back.	
Bind off all	10 stitches

RIGHT FRONT

Work right front same as left
front, but reverse shaping. Bind off
stitches at neck edge in following
manner: Knit 1, slip 1, knit 1, pass
slipped stitch over.

THREE-QUARTER-LENGTH SLEEVES

With smaller needles and color A, cast on	34 stitches
Work in knit-1-purl-1 ribbing for	2-1/2 inches (6cm)

Work in 16-row sequence, beginning
with color A.

Row 1: Knit across row, increasing evenly making total of	20 stitches 54 stitches

Rows 2, 4 and 6: Purl across row.
Rows 3 and 5: Knit across row.
Change to color B.
Row 7: Knit 4 *Knit 1, loop, knit 2, loop,
knit 2, loop, knit 5; repeat from * 5 times.
Row 8: *Purl 5, purl 2 together, purl 1,
purl 2 together, purl 1, purl 2 together;
repeat from * 5 times; end with purl 4.
Row 9 through 16: Work in sequence to
match the back.

Continue to work even until total length of sleeve measures	10-1/2 inches (27cm)
or desired length to underarm.	

Helpful Hint

Don't worry if your knitting is uneven.
Hand knitting is a craft.

Pattern continued on next page.

Helpful Hint

Garter- and stockinette-stitch patterns produce different gauges when knit on the same-size needles. With a stockinette stitch, you might get 5 stitches equal to 1 inch (2-1/2cm). On garter you could get 4-1/2 stitches to an inch. That's why it's important to knit a test swatch *each* time.

Cardigan Pattern

Begin armhole shaping. Work following 2 bind-off rows on same rows of color and pattern as worked on front and back. At beginning of following bind off	2 rows 4 stitches
Decrease 1 stitch at beginning *and* end of next 3 knit rows. This leaves	40 stitches
Work even in pattern until armhole measures from first underarm bind-off.	6 inches (15cm)
To form an even puff, on next wrong-side row, purl 2 stitches together across row. This leaves	20 stitches
On following row, knit 2 stitches together across row.	
Bind off all stitches in pattern.	

FINISHING

Sew back and front shoulders together. To make front bands, with smaller needles and color A, pick up 5 stitches left on holders. Work right- and left-front bands separately. Work in knit-1-purl-1 ribbing until long enough to go up front edge and into middle of back. Bind off. Join both bands at center back. With main color A, sew borders to edge of cardigan. Set in sleeves. Sew underarm and side seams. *Optional:* With color A, work line of single crochet around front border or work an overcast or other decorative stitch.

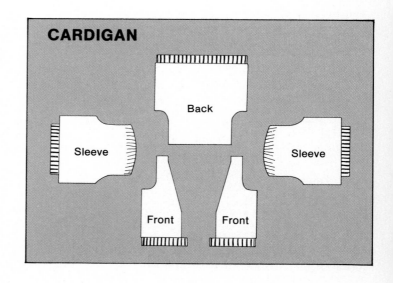

Daisy-Petals Camisole.

Camisole Pattern

Check your gauge to avoid disappointment.

BACK AND FRONT
Make two pieces alike.

With smaller needles and color C used double, cast on	68 stitches
Work in knit-1-purl-1 ribbing for	1 inch (2-1/2cm)
Change to larger needles and work in stockinette stitch for	11 inches (28cm)
or 1 inch (2-1/2cm) less than total desired length.	
On following knit row, change to color B. Work two rows of daisy-petal pattern. Row 1: Knit 8, *knit 1, loop, knit 2, loop, knit 2, loop knit 5; repeat from *	6 times
Row 2: *Purl 5, purl 2 together, purl 1, purl 2 together, purl 1, purl 2 together; repeat from * 6 times. Change to color C. Work 4 rows in stockinette stitch.	
Begin 4 rows of reverse-stockinette stitch for hem. Rows 1 and 3: Purl across row. Rows 2 and 4: Knit across row.	
Bind off loosely in pattern.	

FINISHING
Sew side seams. Fold down hem and tack to garment by catching only backs of stitches. Leave 1/2-inch (1cm) opening for elastic. Measure elastic to fit snugly around chest, and add 1 inch (2-1/2cm). Attach one end of elastic to a safety pin. Push pin and elastic through hem. Remove safety pin. Let both ends of elastic protrude through opening. Overlap them 1 inch (2-1/2cm), and stitch together. Sew hem opening.
Optional: To make shoulder straps, knit or crochet thin shoulder straps or use ribbon.

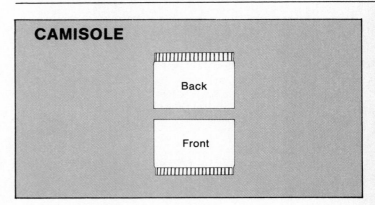

CAMISOLE

Back

Front

Summer-Comfort Sleeveless V-Neck Sweater.

SUMMER-COMFORT SLEEVELESS V-NECK

In warm weather, you'll be cool and comfortable in this top. And it looks great! It's made of two pieces. Increases for the sleeves form a natural roll.

DESIGN YOUR OWN
Make it Dazzling—Work this easy V-neck in metallic yarn. It'll be dressy enough to wear with pants or a summer skirt, but still keep you cool. This sweater is shown in burgundy and metallic gold on the cover.
Summer Wardrobe—Make several tops in different colors and yarns. Be sure you work the correct gauge.
Tunic Length—Add rows for a hip-length tunic to wear with a belt. See *Designing Your Own*, page 120, for instructions.

SUITABLE YARN
Sport-weight cotton, acrylic and blended yarn

YARN SHOWN
Linen-and-cotton mixture *Lin et Cot* by Berger du Nord 50-gram skeins
Color: Beige

YARN SHOWN ON COVER
These two yarns are worked together.
Cotton-and linen *Lino Fino* by Joseph Galler
170 yards = 50 grams
Color: Burgundy
65% Viscose—35% metallized polyester *Gyps' Anny Lurex* by anny blatt
11/16 ounces = 20 grams
Color: Gold

TOOLS AND SUPPLIES
No. 4 and No. 6 needles or sizes to obtain correct gauge

STITCH PATTERNS
Ribbing—*Knit 2, purl 2; repeat from * across every row.
Reverse-Stockinette Stitch—Alternate knit and purl rows. Use grainy texture as the right-side.

GAUGE
Lin et Cot used double, in reverse-stockinette stitch with larger needles:
4 stitches = 1 inch (2-1/2cm)
5 rows = 1 inch (2-1/2cm) approximately

SIZE
Women's small-medium and large.

	Small-Medium	Large
Body chest measurements	31-34 (79-87	36-38 inches 92-97cm)
Knitted chest measurements	35 (89	39 inches 100cm)
Width of knitted front and back	17-1/2 (44	19-1/2 inches 50cm)
Yarn required	5	6 skeins

Pattern

Check your gauge to avoid disappointment.

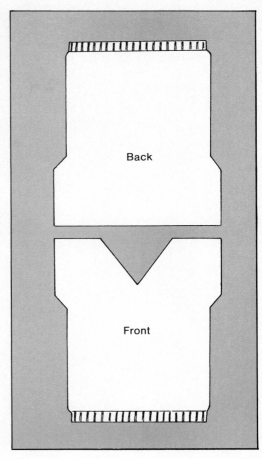

Back

Front

BACK		
On smaller needles, cast on	66	74 stitches
Work in knit-2-purl-2 ribbing for	2-1/2 (6	2-1/2 inches 6cm)
On final row of ribbing, increase evenly across row for total of	4 70	4 stitches 78 stitches
Change to larger needles and reverse-stockinette stitch. Work even until total length measures	13 (33	14 inches 36cm)
or 1 inch (2-1/2cm) less than desired length to underarm.		
On next knit row, begin sleeve shaping. At *both* ends of every knit row, increase	1 5	1 stitch 7 times
for total of	80	92 stitches
Work even until sleeve measures	7 (18	8 inches 20cm)
above final increase.		
Bind off loosely in pattern.		

FRONT		
Work front same as back until sleeve increases are completed. Divide for V-neck. On next knit row, knit over	37	43 stitches
Knit 2 together, knit 1. Attach ball of yarn. Knit 1, slip 1, knit 1 and pass slipped stitch over. Knit over remaining	37	43 stitches
Work both sides of front at the same time with ball of yarn for each side. On each following knit row, decrease along both center edges as described until remain. Work even until front is same length as back.	26	31 stitches
Bind off loosely in pattern.		

FINISHING
Sew shoulder seams, then sew side seams, including increase of stitches for sleeve. Allow sleeves to roll back. Tack sleeves at shoulders.

Portuguese Fisherman's Knit Sweater.

PORTUGUESE FISHERMAN'S KNIT

Generations of Portuguese fisherman have worn this sweater for its warmth and comfort. Native water-repellent wool keeps out dampness and sea spray.

You can find yarns with similar qualities, such as *Icelandic.* The yarn shown is a versatile orlon-acrylic. The gauge of 4 stitches to an inch (2-1/2cm) differs from the usual recommendation. When knitting is complete, add Portuguese-style red duplicate-stitching on the yoke for a good-looking, practical sweater.

DESIGN YOUR OWN

Embroidery—Portuguese women vary decorations on sweaters. You can adapt cross-stitch and other embroidery patterns for the yoke and different areas of the sweater.
Jacquard Patterns—In true Portuguese style, embroidery is knitted into the body of the sweater with a knitting technique. This technique is called *jacquard.* The colored yarn not in use is carried across the back of the work. The graph shown on page 109 for duplicate-stitching on the yoke can be adapted to this method.

GRAPH FOR DUPLICATE-STITCHING

This design is made of a central cross pattern between two double straight lines. A complete design is five stitches wide. Begin embroidery next to the garter border, at the neck opening. Make as many complete designs as possible.

Add broken designs up to the armhole edges, as specified in pattern instructions.

SUITABLE YARN

Worsted-weight acrylic, wool or cotton yarn
Use a compatible yarn for duplicate-stitching

YARN SHOWN

For sweater:
Orlon-acrylic worsted *Windrush* by Brunswick
3-1/2 ounces = 100 grams
Color: Sea oats heather
For duplicate-stitching and tie:
Orlon-acrylic *Minicraft* by Brunswick
25-yard skeins
Color: Bright scarlet

TOOLS AND SUPPLIES

No. 8 and No. 10 needles or sizes to obtain correct gauge

STITCH PATTERNS

Ribbing—*Knit 1, purl 1; repeat from * across every row.
Stockinette Stitch—Alternate rows of knit and purl.

GAUGE

With larger needles, in stockinette stitch:
4 stitches = 1 inch (2-1/2cm)
5 rows = 1 inch (2-1/2cm) approximately

SIZE

Complete size range for children, women and men.

	CHILDREN			WOMEN			MEN		
	Small	Medium	Large	Small	Medium	Large	Small	Medium	Large
Body chest measurements	23-24 (59-61	26-28 66-71	30 76	30-31 76-79	32-34 82-87	36-38 92-97	38-40 97-102	42-44 107-112	46 inches 117cm)
Knitted chest measurements	26 (66	29 74	32 82	33 84	36 92	39 100	41 104	45 115	48 inches 122cm)
Width of knitted front and back	13 (33	14-1/2 37	16 40	16-1/2 42	18 46	19-1/2 50	20-1/2 52	22-1/2 57	24 inches 61cm)
Sleeve length—wrist to underarm	11 (28	13 33	15 38	17 43	18 46	18-1/2 47	19 48	19-1/2 50	21-1/2 inches 55cm)
Length from beginning to shoulder	14 (36	16 40	18 46	21 54	22 56	23 59	25 64	26 66	28 inches 71cm)
Yarn required:									
Worsted-weight	3	3	3	4	5	5	6	7	7 skeins
Red embroidery yarn	1	1	1	2	2	2	2	2	2 skeins

Pattern

Check your gauge to avoid disappointment.

BACK

With smaller needles, cast on	52	58	64	66	72	78	82	90	96 stitches
Work in knit-1-purl-1 ribbing for	2 (5	2 5	2 5	2-1/2 6	2-1/2 6	2-1/2 6	3 8	3 8	3 inches 8cm)
Change to larger needles and stockinette stitch. Work even for total length of or desired length to armhole.	9 (22	10 25	11-1/2 29	14 36	14-1/2 37	15 38	16-1/2 42	17 43	18 inches 46cm)
Armhole is not shaped, but begin garter-stitch border along both armhole edges to shoulder, as follows: Every row, knit *first* and *last* 6 stitches. On center stitches, continue in stockinette stitch. Work even until total length measures	13-1/2 (34	15-1/2 39	17-1/2 44	21 54	22 56	23 59	25 64	26 66	28 inches 71cm)

Bind off loosely in pattern.

FRONT

Work front same as back to armholes where garter borders begin.
Divide front in half for neck opening. Work each side separately with a 6-stitch band of garter stitch on both neckline and armhole edges. Stockinette stitch is worked between borders.

Pattern continued on next page.

Portuguese Fisherman's Knit	CHILDREN			WOMEN			MEN		
	Small	Medium	Large	Small	Medium	Large	Small	Medium	Large
This makes total of	26	29	32	33	36	39	41	45	48 stitches
Continue in established pattern until total length of front measures same as back. Bind off loosely in pattern.									
DUPLICATE-STITCHING See graph. Total number of cross patterns to be stitched	2	3	4	4	4	5	5	6	7 patterns
plus extra stitches of broken pattern to reach armhole edges	4	2	0	1	4	2	1	3	1 stitches
SHOULDER SEAMS Divide back into thirds for two shoulders and neck. Sew back and front shoulders together. Match number of stitches.									
NECKBAND With smaller needles, pick up on left front	9	10	11	11	12	13	14	15	16 stitches
on back neck	18	20	22	22	24	26	28	30	32 stitches
on right front	9	10	11	11	12	13	14	15	16 stitches
for total of	36	40	44	44	48	52	56	60	64 stitches
Work in knit-1-purl-1 ribbing for 1 inch (2-1/2cm).									
Bind off loosely in pattern.									
SLEEVES With smaller needles, cast on	22	30	36	38	40	42	44	48	48 stitches
Work in knit-1-purl-1 ribbing for	2 (5	2 5	2 5	2-1/2 6	2-1/2 6	2-1/2 6	3 8	3 8	3 inches 8cm)
Change to larger needles and stockinette stitch. Increase 1 stitch at *each* end of row every inch	7	7	8	9	10	11	11	12	13 times
for total of	36	44	50	56	60	64	68	72	78 stitches
Work even until sleeve measures	11 (28	13 33	15 38	17 43	18 46	18-1/2 47	19 48	19-1/2 50	21-1/2 inches 55cm)
or desired length.									
Bind off loosely in pattern.									

Pattern continued in next page.

FINISHING

Sew underarm and side seams. Crochet tie about 30 inches (76cm) long for children and 50 inches (128cm) for adults. Lace through front opening. Cross at 1-inch (2-1/2cm) intervals. Stitches should be loose enough to permit cord to be pulled through.

Optional: Reinforce holes with overstitching. Tie cord in a bow after sweater is slipped over the head. Tie knots at both ends of the cord. If necessary, cut ends shorter.

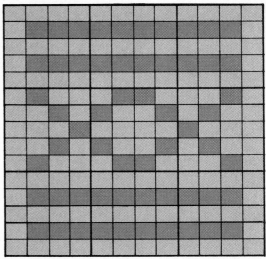

Duplicate-stitching pattern for design.

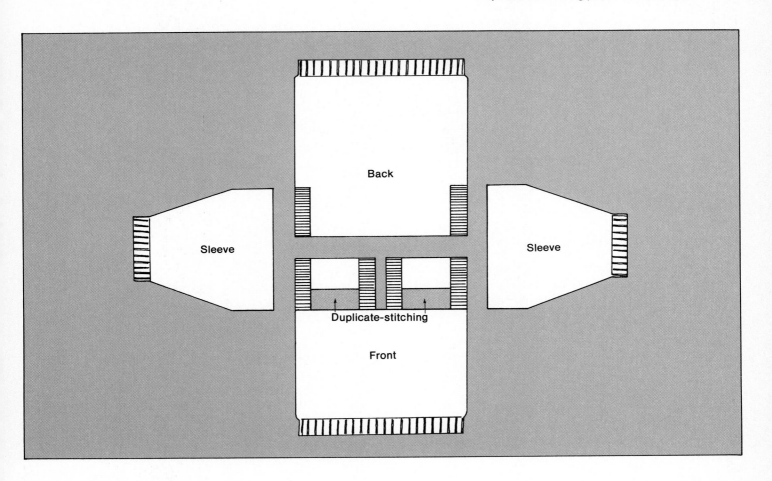

Bobbles-and-Waffles Sweater.

BOBBLES AND WAFFLES

Wear this as a jacket, or button it up and wear it as a sweater. Either way, this garment will be a sweater you'll love.

The dropped shoulder is outlined with a row of bobble stitches that continues across the yoke. Bobbles are knobs made by knitting back and forth into one stitch. They're fun to knit. See page 27 for more information on making bobbles.

Any worsted-weight yarn is suitable. *Trilla* was chosen for the sweater in the photo. The loft of Trilla brings out the sculptural contrast of the different stitches used in this pattern. *Loft* is the amount of air in the yarn that contributes to a full-bodied look.

DESIGN YOUR OWN
Short-Sleeve Version—Make this cardigan pattern with short sleeves. Knit the back and front as shown. For sleeves, cast on 80 (85) stitches.
Rows 1 to 4: *Knit 1, purl 1; repeat from * across every row.
Row 2: Knit across row.
Row 3: Purl across row.
Row 4: Work bobbles same as for the top of the cardigan sleeve.
Row 5: Purl across row.
Bind off loosely in pattern.

SUITABLE YARN
Worsted-weight wool, cotton or acrylic yarn

YARN SHOWN
100% wool *88-Line Trilla* by Textile Studios
125 yards = 64 grams
Color: Peacock blue

TOOLS AND SUPPLIES
No. 5 and No. 7 needles or sizes to obtain correct gauge
3 stitch holders
1 ring marker
6 buttons, 3/4 inch (2cm) in diameter

STITCH PATTERNS
Ribbing—Knit 1, purl 1; repeat from * across every row.
Stockinette Stitch—Alternate knit and purl rows.
Bobbles—Repeat this pattern to make one bobble:
   In one stitch: knit 1, yarn over, knit 1, turn to wrong-side; purl 3, turn to right-side; knit 3, turn to wrong-side; purl 3, turn to right-side; slip 1, knit 2 together, pass slipped stitch over.
Waffle Stitch—Repeat this pattern over four rows.
   Row 1: *Knit 2, purl 1; repeat from * across row.
   Row 2: *Knit 1, purl 2; repeat from * across row.
   Row 3: Same as row 1.
   Row 4: Knit across row.

GAUGE
With larger needles, in stockinette stitch:
5 stitches = 1 inch (2-1/2cm)
6 rows = 1 inch (2-1/2cm) approximately

SIZE
Women's small-medium and large.

	Small-Medium	Large
Body chest measurements	32-34 (82-87	36-38 inches 92-97cm)
Knitted chest measurements	36 (92	39 inches 100cm)
Width of knitted front and back	18 (46	19-1/2 inches 50cm)
Sleeve length—wrist to underarm	18 (46	19 inches 48cm)
Length from beginning to shoulder	21-1/2 (55	23-1/2 inches 60cm)
Yarn required	7	8 skeins

Helpful Hint

Textured stitch patterns show up better in light-color yarns than in dark shades.

Pattern

Check your gauge to avoid disappointment.

	Small-Medium	Large
BACK With smaller needles, cast on	85	93 stitches
Work in knit-1-purl-1 ribbing for	2-1/2 (5	2-1/2 inches 5cm)
Change to larger needles. On the first knit row, increase	5	5 stitches
evenly spaced across row for total of	90	98 stitches
On following row, work bobbles. *Knit 3, make bobble in next stitch; repeat from * across;	22	24 times
End row with knit 2. Work even in stockinette stitch until total length measures	21 (54	23 inches 59cm)
or approximately 1/2 inch (1cm) less than desired length to shoulder.		
Shape shoulders. On following knit row, for right shoulder knit	28	30 stitches
turn and purl	28	30 stitches
turn and knit	28	30 stitches
Bind these stitches off loosely.		
For back of neck, place on holder	34	38 stitches
For left shoulder, attach new yarn at neck edge. Work to match right shoulder.	28	30 stitches
LEFT FRONT With smaller needles, cast on	48	51 stitches
Work in knit-1-purl-1 ribbing over	41	44 stitches
Place marker on needle and work in garter stitch over remaining This establishes front border.	7	7 stitches
Work in ribbing-and-garter pattern for	2-1/2 (6	2-1/2 inches 6cm)

Pattern continued on next page.

Bobbles and Waffles	Small-Medium	Large
Change to larger needles. *Maintain 7-stitch garter border for entire front up to neckline.* On first knit row, increase evenly spaced across row, for total of	4 52	4 stitches 55 stitches
Purl next row. On following row, work bobbles. Knit	1	0 stitch
*Make bobble in next stitch, knit 3; repeat from * across	11	12 times
Continue working in stockinette stitch for or desired length to underarm.	14 (36	15 inches 38cm)
On following knit row, work bobbles same as before above ribbing. Purl next row.		
Begin waffle pattern over repeating 4-row sequence for	45 4 (10	48 stitches 4-1/2 inches 12cm)
Shape neckline. Beginning with next right-side row, work in waffle pattern over	28	30 stitches
Place on holder for neck front remaining	24	25 stitches
Work in waffle pattern over until front measures same to shoulders as back. Bind off loosely in pattern.	28	30 stitches

BUTTON PLACEMENT
Sew six buttons to center of garter border as follows: Sew 1 button 1/2 inch (1cm) from bottom edge, 1 button 1 inch (2-1/2cm) below neck edge, 4 buttons spaced evenly in between, approximately 3-1/2 inches (9cm) apart.

RIGHT FRONT
Work right front same as left front, but reverse shaping. Make six buttonholes to correspond to button placement on left front. Work buttonholes on garter border as follows: On right-side row: Knit 2, bind off 3, knit 2.
On following row: Knit 2, cast on 3, knit 2.

SLEEVES
Make two sleeves alike.

	Small-Medium	Large
With smaller needles, cast on	42	45 stitches
Work in knit-1-purl-1 ribbing for	2 (5	2 inches 5cm)
Change to larger needles. On first knit row, increase	12	14 stitches
evenly spaced across row for total of Purl next row.	54	59 stitches
On the following row work bobbles. Knit	2	3 stitches

Pattern continued on next page.

Bobbles and Waffles	Small-Medium	Large
*Make bobble in next stitch, knit 3; repeat from * across. Continue to work in stockinette stitch, increasing 1 stitch at both ends of every 6th row	13	14 times
for total of	80	85 stitches
Work even until total length of sleeve measures	18 (46	19 inches 48cm)
or 1/2 inch (1cm) less than desired length to underarm.		
On following knit row, work bobbles: Knit	4	1 stitches
*Make bobble in next stitch, knit 3; repeat from * across row	19	21 times
Purl next row.		
Bind off all stitches loosely.		

FINISHING
Sew shoulder seams. Match front and sleeve bobbles, and set in sleeves. Sew side and underarm seams.

NECKBAND
With right-side facing you, pick up

	Small-Medium	Large
from right-front holder	24	25 stitches
from vertical right-front edge	14	16 stitches
from center-back holder	34	38 stitches
from vertical left-front edge	14	16 stitches
from left-front holder	24	25 stitches
for total of	110	120 stitches

Work in knit-1-purl-1 ribbing, except work garter stitch on first and last 7 border stitches as follows: On next right-side row begin buttonhole as instructed for right front. On following row, complete buttonhole. Work even in established pattern until neckband measures 1 inch (2-1/2cm). Bind off loosely in pattern. Sew button on left-front neckband.

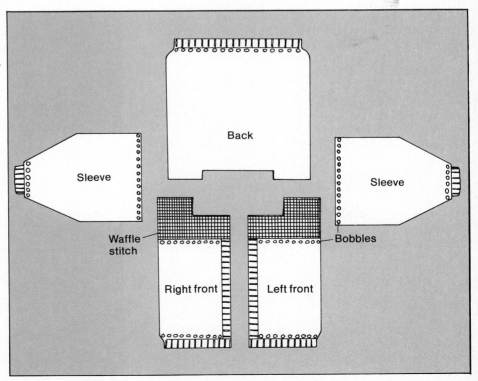

Back

Sleeve

Sleeve

Waffle stitch

Bobbles

Right front

Left front

The Ultimate Sweatshirt.

THE ULTIMATE SWEATSHIRT

Combine the comfort of an old sweatshirt with the texture of an unusual yarn—you'll have a winner. *Boucle* is a thick-and-thin yarn that knits into a pebbly texture. Suggested needle sizes are smaller than you might expect for similar-weight yarn. Bumps in the yarn force you to knit more loosely. Be sure you knit true to gauge.

Instructions are given for women's medium size only. This oversize style will fit smaller and larger sizes, as indicated under *Size* measurements.

DESIGN YOUR OWN

Evening Glitter—Make a dressier sweatshirt by knitting with metallic yarn. Or overstitch armhole seams with gold or silver yarn to match jewelry.

Color Breaks—Work the pattern in two colors as follows: Back and front: with color A, work ribbing. With color B, work up to armhole decreases. With color A, work remaining length to shoulders. For the sleeves, work all in color A.

Other Colors—Here are some suggested color combinations: peach and white; lilac and turquoise; black and gray. Use your imagination to create other color combinations.

SUITABLE YARN

Worsted-weight yarn

YARN SHOWN

Blended yarn *Calico Boucle* by Bernat
1-3/4 ounces = 50 grams
Color: Raspberry

TOOLS AND SUPPLIES

No. 3 and No. 6 needles or sizes to obtain correct gauge

STITCH PATTERNS

Ribbing—*Knit 1, purl 1; repeat from * across every row.
Stockinette Stitch—Alternating rows of knit and purl.

GAUGE

With larger needles, in stockinette stitch:
4 stitches = 1 inch (2-1/2cm)
5 rows = 1 inch (2-1/2cm) approximately

SIZE

Women's medium.

Body chest measurements	32-36 inches (82-92cm)
Knitted chest measurements	40 inches (102cm)
Width of knitted back and front	20 inches (51cm)
Three-quarter-length sleeve to underarm	14-1/2 inches (37cm)
Length from beginning to shoulder	23 inches (59cm)
Yarn required	13 skeins

Pattern continued on next page.

Pattern

Check your gauge to avoid disappointment.

BACK

With smaller needles, cast on	66 stitches
Work in knit-1-purl-1 ribbing for	3 inches (8cm)
Change to larger needles and stockinette stitch. Increase evenly across first row for total of	18 stitches 84 stitches
Work even until total length measures or desired length to underarm.	13 inches (33cm)

Length to underarm measures about 1-1/2 inches (4cm) less than usual because of deep armhole.

At beginning of next 2 rows, bind off	18 stitches
This leaves	48 stitches
Work even until armhole measures	9 inches (22cm)

End with a purl row.

Begin neck shaping. On next right-side row, knit across	6 stitches
Place on holder for center neck remaining	36 stitches
Attach new yarn, and knit over remaining	6 stitches

On both shoulders, work 3 rows of stockinette stitch.

Bind off loosely in pattern.

FRONT

Work front same as back until armhole measures	8 inches (20cm)

Shape center neck the same as for back. Work shoulder pieces 1 inch (2-1/2cm) longer. Front will be same total length as back.

For each shoulder, loosely bind off remaining	6 stitches

SLEEVES

With smaller needles, cast on	40 stitches
Work in knit-1-purl-1 ribbing for	5 inches (13cm)
Change to larger needles and stockinette stitch. Increase 1 stitch in *every* stitch across row for total of	80 stitches
Continue even until total length of sleeve measures	19 inches (48cm)

or 4-1/2 inches (12cm) longer than desired length to underarm.

Bind off loosely in pattern.

Pattern continued in next column.

FINISHING

Sew right shoulder seam only.
Neckband is worked with smaller needles in knit-1-purl-1 ribbing. With right-side of work facing you, pick up and work in pattern as follows:

From left-front-neck edge	8 stitches
from front holder	36 stitches
from right-front-neck edge	8 stitches
from right-back-neck edge	4 stitches
from back holder	36 stitches
from left-back-neck edge	4 stitches
for total of	96 stitches
Work in ribbing for	1 inch (2-1/2cm)

Bind off loosely in pattern.

Seam together left shoulder and neckband. Lay all pieces on a flat surface. Upper, bound-off edge of each sleeve matches the length of vertical edge of armhole. Corners of sleeves fit exactly into front and back. See illustration below. Sew in sleeves. Sew underarm and side seams.

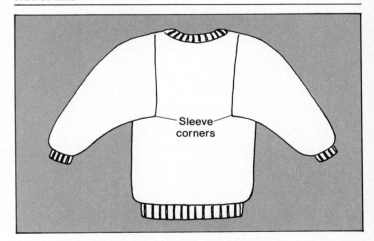

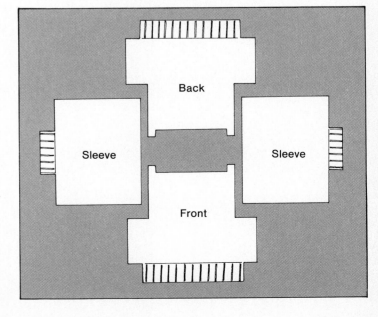

SUPERCAPE

Is it a cape? Is it a shawl? Is it a poncho? It's whatever you want it to be—casual one minute, elegant the next. It goes over jeans as well as cool summer dresses and fits comfortably over winter jackets.

The pattern is made of two pieces. Left and right sides are knitted from the front, over the shoulders, into a pointed back.

DESIGN YOUR OWN
Drama—For dramatic flair, make the supercape in black worsted yarn, used double. Work glittering metallic yarn along the six edge stitches and into the tassels.

SUITABLE YARN
Bulky-weight yarn or worsted-weight yarn, used double

YARN SHOWN
60% wool-40% mohair *Harmonieuse* by Joseph Galler
74 yards = 75 grams
Color: Blue variegated

TOOLS AND SUPPLIES
No. 10-1/2 needles or size to obtain correct gauge

STITCH PATTERNS
Stockinette Stitch—Alternate knit and purl rows.
Seed Stitch—This stitch is used for pockets and borders.
Every row: *Knit 1, purl 1; repeat from * across every row, end with knit 1.

GAUGE
In stockinette stitch:
10-1/2 stitches = 4 inches (10cm)
4 rows = 1 inch (2-1/2cm) approximately

SIZE
One size fits all.

YARN REQUIRED
10 skeins

Pattern

Check your gauge to avoid disappointment.

RIGHT SIDE

Cast on	35 stitches
Work in seed stitch for	3 inches (8cm)
On next row, establish borders in seed stitch over the first *and* last	6 stitches
Work the center in stockinette stitch over	23 stitches
Work even in established pattern until total length measures	23 inches (59cm)
On right-side edge, increase 1 stitch every 4th row, between seed-stitch border and stockinette stitch for total of	10 times 45 stitches

Pattern continued in next column.

On following 4th row, increase at *both* sides between seed-stitch border and stockinette stitch.	1 stitch
Continue increasing every 4th row for total of	6 times 59 stitches

On next knit row, begin shaping back point by decreasing at *both* edges simultaneously.
On left inside edge, decrease 1 stitch at beginning of every knit row   6 times

This eliminates seed border.
At the same time, on right side, decrease 1 stitch between border and stockinette stitch on *every* knit row until 6 stitches of border remain.

Continue decreasing every other left-side row in seed pattern, until all stitches are bound off.

LEFT SIDE
Work left side same as right side, but reverse shaping.

FINISHING
Fold up 8-inch (20cm) pockets, and sew sides. Sew middle seam to form point for back. Make a 6-inch (15cm) tassel and sew to back point. Make four 4-inch tassels (10cm). Sew them to the bottom of pockets. Instructions for tassels are found on page 20. Sew tassels on with light-weight yarn or heavy thread. Bulky knitting yarn can be difficult to work with.

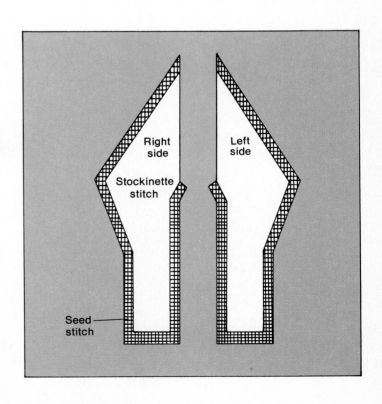

Designing Your Own

Knitting is fun! When you finish a sweater, you have accomplished something. After you master following pattern directions, consider taking the craft a step further by *designing your own* garments. It could become the most satisfying part of your knitting.

Start by adapting an existing pattern to suit you. If you have tried some of the variations given in the *Design Your Own* section of the patterns, you've already done some designing. Many well-known designers gained experience this way and went on to create their own fashions.

DESIGN OBJECTIVES

In making design adaptations, you'll be able to create a piece of clothing to:
- Fit your figure.
- Reflect your individual taste.
- Cater to changing fashion trends.

WHAT MAKES KNITTING CLICK

It may be helpful to understand how to choose a pattern and yarn for a project. You usually look for a pattern that is attractive and stylish, of the correct size and fit. You also look for yarn in colors you like and stitch patterns with appealing textures.

These are the components of any garment you make. When you look for a pattern, you are hoping to find one that has the right combination of these features. In this section, you'll learn how to change each component to suit you.

SHAPE

PARTS OF A SWEATER OR JACKET

Knitting patterns, like sewing patterns, are constructed of basic pieces. The standard parts for sweaters, jackets and other tops are:
- The body—back and front.
- Sleeves.
- Options, such as neckbands, collars, hoods.

It's possible to group the combination of these various shapes into three categories. These are *block shapes, traditional shapes* and *combinations of both.*

BLOCK SHAPES

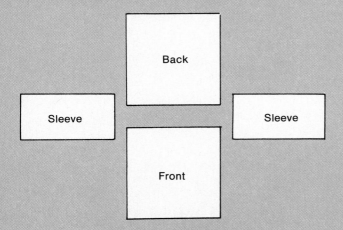

BLOCK SHAPES

All parts of block shapes are plain rectangles. In a block knit, you cast on a specified number of stitches. You knit a certain length, then bind off the same number of stitches. This method is the simplest way to knit. Block knits produce easy-fitting garments. See illustration in previous column.

TRADITIONAL SHAPES

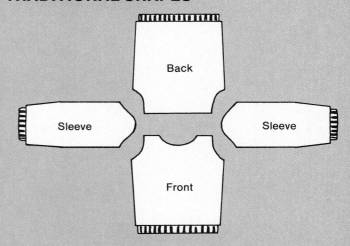

TRADITIONAL SHAPES

Pieces are tapered, and armholes and necklines are indented. To achieve these shapes, you are given the number of stitches to cast on, then instructed where to increase and decrease as you work. You have control over the fit of a garment—it can fit close to the body or be loose. See illustration above.

COMBINATION OF BLOCK AND TRADITIONAL SHAPES

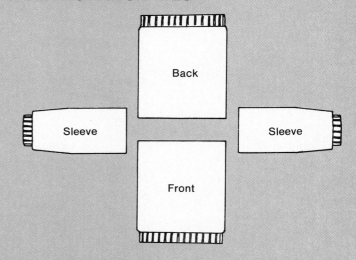

COMBINATION OF BLOCK AND TRADITIONAL

A block body may be combined with tapered sleeves or vice versa. Other possibilities also exist. See illustration above.

MAKE IT LONGER, MAKE IT SHORTER

Lengthening or shortening may be required to adjust for long- or short-waisted people, long or short arms or because you like things longer. Make these adjustments, when possible, on a *straight* stretch, while you are working even. This means you don't increase or decrease at the edges. Insert the required inches and continue with pattern instructions. Lengthening requires extra yarn.

CHANGING BACK AND FRONT PATTERNS

Increase or reduce the length between the ribbing and underarm. Waist ribbing remains the same. Add or subtract the required number of inches to the measurement specified to the armhole. In block knitting, add or subtract from the measurement given from ribbing to the shoulder.

LENGTHEN A SWEATER INTO A TUNIC

Sweaters can be made as tunics or dresses by adding length to the body. This can be done with the *Playing with Blocks* sweater, page 65. Check the knitted measurement given for the *widest* part of the pattern. Be sure it provides enough room for hips. See illustration below.

Work ribbing on needles one or two sizes larger than you use for the body. Ribbing is designed to contract around the waist. Large needles keep ribbing from contracting around the hips.

SWEATER INTO TUNIC

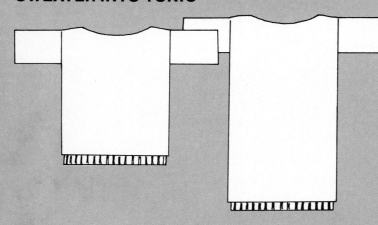

TURN A JACKET INTO A COAT

Decide how much extra length is required to make a knee-length or full-length coat. Add the required length to the back and front. These alterations are recommended *only* for straight line patterns, not flared designs. Try this variation with the *Bobbles-and-Waffles* sweater, page 110. See illustration in next column.

MAKE A VEST INTO A TUNIC

Add length to a straight, hip-length vest, and it becomes a long tunic. This can be done with the *Short Vest*, page 52.

JACKET INTO COAT

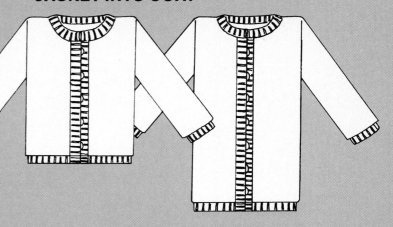

SHORTEN SWEATER OR JACKET

Shorten a sweater or jacket pattern into a waist-length or midriff sweater or bolero. Subtract inches from the body to make the sweater shorter.

CHANGE SLEEVE LENGTHS

Sleeves are lengthened and shortened the same way as body pieces. Lengthening is done between ribbing and the armhole.

Block-Knitted Sleeves—In block knitting, knit the desired sleeve length. Change long sleeves to short sleeves or short sleeves to long sleeves.

BLOCK SLEEVES

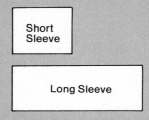

Short into Long—To turn a tapered short sleeve into a long sleeve, determine the wrist measurement first. Convert this wrist measurement into stitches by using the gauge on your test swatch. Cast on the calculated number of stitches. After the ribbing, increase one stitch at both ends of every *fifth* row until you have the number of stitches required at the armhole. Work the sleeves even. Continue with short-sleeve pattern instructions when you reach the armhole.

TAPERED SLEEVES

Long into Short—Convert a long sleeve into a short sleeve. Determine how many stitches to cast on for the bottom of the sleeve. Use the number of stitches specified at the armhole of the long-sleeve pattern. Cast on the same number of stitches. Work in ribbing for 1 to 1-1/4 inches (2-1/2 to 3cm) or as desired. Knit even for the desired length to the underarm. Continue with the long-sleeve pattern.

If you want to make ribbing a little tighter, cast on fewer stitches. Add the number you did not cast on evenly across the row when you begin the main stitch pattern.

Adding Cuffs—For turned-up cuffs, add 2 inches (5 cm) or whatever length you desire.

MAKE IT FIT

WIDER BODY

To achieve a looser fit, you may be able to select the next larger size. You may find after checking all the measurements the whole garment will be too big. Stay with the proper size. Add extra stitches to the back and front, but leave the sleeve pattern unchanged. Patterns include 2 inches (5 cm) more than actual body measurements to allow for movement. See illustration below.

On Block Knitteds—Decide how much you want to add to the back and front. Work with the stitch gauge to find out how many extra stitches you need. Adding 1 inch (2-1/2cm) to the back and 1 inch (2-1/2cm) to the front means you're adding 2 inches (5cm) all around.

On Shaped Pieces—With shaped pieces, you add extra stitches the same way as for block knitteds. Decrease for the armholes as instructed in the pattern. When you reach the shoulder line, add extra stitches evenly over the center neck and both shoulders.

WIDER BODY

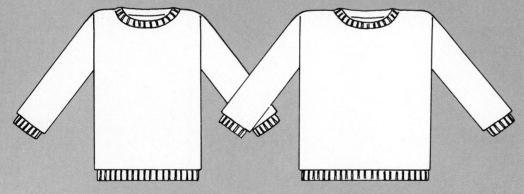

SLIMMER BODY

If you want a tighter-fitting garment, select a smaller size. Check the sleeve length to be sure it is correct. It's easy to knit sleeves a bit longer, if necessary.

SHOULDER ADJUSTMENTS

To change shoulder widths, make minor adjustments at the armhole. For wider shoulders, increase a few stitches at the vertical edge of the armhole. For narrower shoulders, decrease between the underarm and shoulders. Calculate the number of stitches to add or subtract by referring to the stitch gauge.

MAKE IT DIFFERENT

TURN A SWEATER INTO A JACKET

Change the pattern for the front of a pullover sweater into a jacket or cardigan. Divide the number of stitches for the sweater by two. If you want overlapping bands of six stitches, cast on three extra stitches on the button side and three extra stitches on the buttonhole side. Knit a band six stitches wide on both center edges. This could be done with the sweater *Simply Striped,* page 49.

TURN A CARDIGAN INTO A VEST

To turn a cardigan into a vest, omit the sleeves. If you want to, crochet around the armholes for an attractive finish and to keep edges from curling under. Try this on the *Bobbles-and-Waffles* sweater, page 110. See illustration below.

CARDIGAN INTO VEST

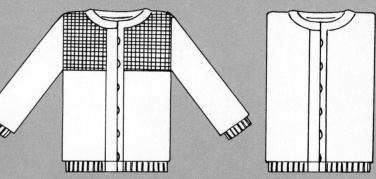

ADD A TURTLENECK

A *turtleneck* is a tube made of two rectangles sewn together along the long edges. It is usually knitted in ribbing for a good fit and to allow enough room to slide over your head.

A turtleneck can be knitted without interruption from the front and back of the garment. This is shown in the *Ribbed Turtleneck,* page 55. The two rectangles can be worked separately and sewn to a round neckline. This could be done on the *Varsity-Letter Sweater,* page 70.

SIDE SLITS

Side slits can be made on the side seams of tunics, sweaters and skirts. When you're putting the garment together, determine the size of the slit. Leave that amount unsewn. Over-stitch both edges of the slit so they lie flat.

TEXTURE

Texture is created with different yarns and stitch patterns. When choosing one yarn over another, you are expressing a texture preference. Compare how one sweater would look if it were knitted in worsted, mohair or boucle yarn.

Stitch patterns offer the best opportunity for creating surface textures. Most knitting patterns combine at least two different stitches—ribbing and the main stitch. There is no reason you can't incorporate three or more stitch varieties in one garment.

Make the body in one stitch and sleeves in another. Or make the main body in one stitch and a yoke in another. Knit the left half of the sweater in a different stitch.

Changing the size of the needles is another way to change surface texture. Knitting a fine yarn with thick needles creates a lacy fabric.

Illustrations below offer some ideas to help you create interesting textures and possibilities of combining them.

TEXTURING POSSIBILITIES

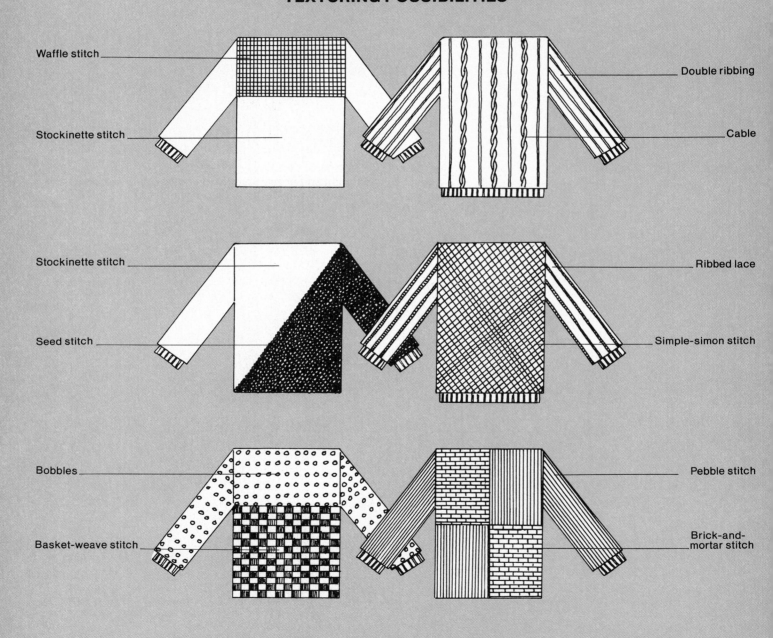

Waffle stitch

Stockinette stitch

Double ribbing

Cable

Stockinette stitch

Seed stitch

Ribbed lace

Simple-simon stitch

Bobbles

Basket-weave stitch

Pebble stitch

Brick-and-mortar stitch

HOW TEXTURE IS CREATED	HOW TEXTURE IS CHANGED
With yarns	• By substituting a different yarn than specified in a pattern. • By using two or more yarns in one garment, such as worsted-weight yarn and mohair yarn. • By using yarn double. • By knitting two different-color yarns as one to create a tweed effect.
With stitch patterns	• By substituting different stitch patterns than specified in a knitting pattern. • By using one or more stitches in sections of a garment. Examples of sectioning include main body and sleeves, main body and yoke, dividing the front vertically down the middle, dividing the front vertically into thirds, knitting stripes in different stitches.
By needle size	• By using smaller needles for tighter fabric. • By using larger needles for looser fabric.

COLOR

With the variety of beautiful yarns available, you may have a hard time choosing between several colors. Try combining two or more colors in one garment. Use the ideas here to help you find colors that look good together. When working with more than one color, use yarns from one manufacturer. As you read the following information, refer to the color wheels on page 124.

TWO-COLOR COMBINATIONS

Analogous Colors—On a color wheel, colors are arranged in a circle. You are always safe using two colors next to each other, which are called *analogous.*

Complementary Colors—Select colors opposite each other on the color wheel. They produce strong contrasts. For example, Christmas green and bright red are a strong contrast.

Primary Colors—The three primary colors—red, blue and yellow—can be used in any combination.

Intensity—Try to keep the intensity of both yarns equal. Peach and lemon are pale versions of orange and yellow.

Monochromatic Schemes—One color in different strengths looks good. Consider light blue with dark blue or spring green with forest green.

Muted Colors—Muted colors work well together, such as dusty rose and olive green.

THREE-COLOR COMBINATIONS

In combining three colors, selection becomes trickier, but some rules hold true. Always hold three balls of yarn together to see whether they please you.

Monochromatic—One-color schemes also work well. Going from a light to a dark shade, or vice versa, is called *ombering.* This type of scheme gives a subtle, chic look to any garment. Think of ombering white, gray and black or beige, tan and brown. Any other color can be ombered if three suitable shades of yarn are available.

Neutral Colors—Neutral colors, such as black, white, gold or silver can be added to any two-color scheme. This often adds drama to an outfit.

Established Schemes—Adopt an established color scheme from a favorite dress, a piece of fabric or wallpaper. Designers have worked out good color combinations you can borrow.

MULTICOLORS

If you want many colors, consider working stripes of equal width. They usually balance in a pleasing arrangement.

TRUST YOUR EYE

The most important point about color is: *If it pleases you, it's probably a good color combination, even if it breaks all the rules.*

COLOR WHEELS

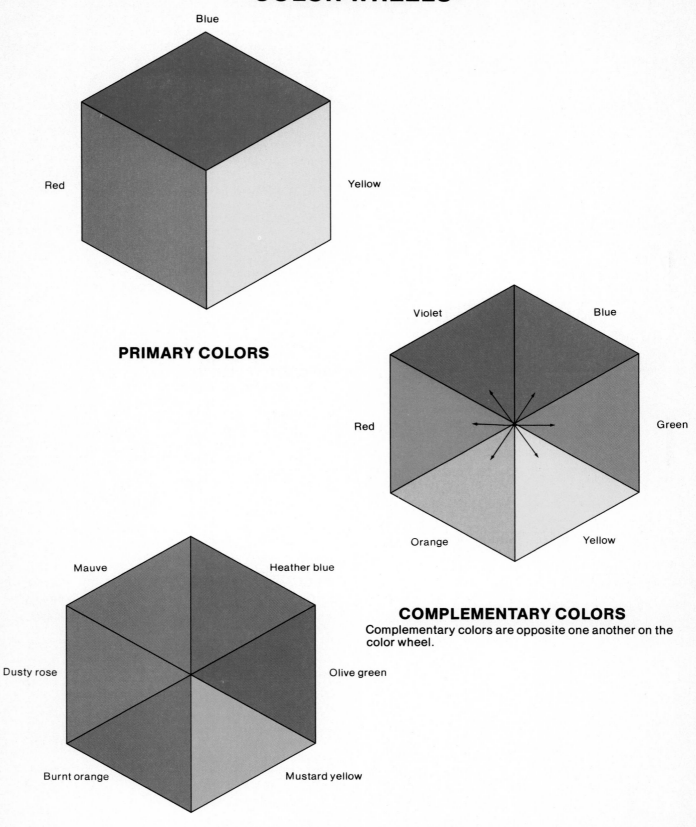

Blue

Red

Yellow

PRIMARY COLORS

Violet

Blue

Red

Green

Orange

Yellow

COMPLEMENTARY COLORS
Complementary colors are opposite one another on the color wheel.

Mauve

Heather blue

Dusty rose

Olive green

Burnt orange

Mustard yellow

MUTED COLORS

Acknowledgments

Special thanks to Aline B. Sosne, a talented young designer who worked closely with the author. Her knowledge of knitting, freely given, proved invaluable. Her original knitting patterns add immeasurably to the book. She is shown in the photo on page 98 modeling the *Daisy-Petals Ensemble,* which is her own creation.

DESIGNERS

FLORENCE TEMKO
A-Line Skirt, All-Occasion T-Shirt, Baby Blanket, Baby Bootie-Mitts, Barbie's Sweater, Canine Coat, Child's Jacket, Friendly Monster Puppet, Super Headband, Ken's Scarf, Leg Warmers, Loopy Afghan, Potholders, Santa's Slipper Socks, Star Hat, Sweater Coat, Pullover Vest.

ALINE B. SOSNE
Baby Bunting, Black-and-White Zigzag, Bobbles and Waffles, Daisy-Petals Ensemble, Here Comes the Gang, Short Vest, Playing with Blocks, Ribbed Turtleneck, Simply Striped, Summer-Comfort, Red, White and Blue, The Ultimate Sweatshirt, Tri-Cable, Varsity-Letter Sweater, Year-Round Favorite.

FLORENCE TEMKO AND ALINE B. SOSNE
Hug-Me, Portuguese Fisherman's Knit.

JOSEPH GALLER, INC.
Butterfly Jacket, Supercape.

KNITTERS

Wynne Alexander, Joan Anyon, Yolanda Anyon (5 years old), Doris Berger, Lena Bergeron, Barbara Bird, Grace Bradford, Shirley Burton, Veronica Durie, Jeanne Gatten, Barbara Griffin, Ursula Haddad, Linna Herman, Juliet Luiks, Sharon Malumphy, Alice Morin, Mary Myers, Caroline Ollivier (9 years old), Stella Pero, Lillian Rosenzweig, Pat Scase, Ruth Silber, Mary Simmons, Mundi Smithers, Aline B. Sosne, Cindy Struss, Florence Temko, Kelly Tripp, Alice White.

MODELS

Pamela Bancroft, Joanna Bendheim, Tamara Bonar, Mercedes Girona, Heidi (dog), Mary-Jane Marinakis, Bonnie Nolan, John Arthur Nolan, Caroline Ollivier, Thomas Ollivier, Deborah Pero, Olana Ragi, Janet Ryan, Aline B. Sosne, Ellen Geis Temko, Janet Temko.

ILLUSTRATIONS

ILLUSTRATIONS
Florence Temko and Doug Burton.
Drawings in *Learning to Knit* section from illustrations in Coats & Clark's Book No. 190-B, *Learn to Knit,* Copyright 1968, Coats & Clark, Inc. 28th edition and duPont's pamphlet, *I Don't Know How to Knit or Crochet Guide,* by E.I duPont de Nemours & Co.

PHOTOGRAPHER
Mike Zwerling.
Photographs taken at *Wheatleigh,* Lenox, Massachusetts and other locations.

Index

Buyer's Guide

**NATURAL-FIBER YARNS
RETAIL AND MAIL ORDER**
Tanglewool (Aline B. Sosne)
83 Church Street
P.O. Box 695
Lenox, MA 01240

YARN MANUFACTURERS AND WHOLESALERS
The following companies will supply names of yarn stores near you:
Anny Blatt Yarns
2477 Crestview Ct.
Farmington Hills, MI 48018
Berger du Nord
Brookman & Sons, Inc.
4872 NE 12th Avenue
Ft. Lauderdale, FL 33334
Bernat Yarn & Craft Corporation
Uxbridge, MA 01569
Brunswick Worsted Mills, Inc.
P.O. Box 276
Pickens, SC 29671
Bucilla Yarns
P.O. Box 1534
Secaucus, NJ 07094
Candide Yarns
100 Main Street South
Woodbury, CT 06798
Coats & Clark Yarns
72 Cummings Point Road
Stamford, CT 06902
Columbia-Minerva Yarns
Customer Service
Box 300
Rochelle, IL 61068
Joseph Galler, Inc.
27 West 20th Street
New York, NY 10011
Tahki Yarns
92 Kennedy Street
Hackensack, NJ 07601
Textile Studios, Inc
26 Union Street
Worth Adams, MA 01247
Zigana Yarn
Kendex Corporation
31332 Via Colinas, No. 107
Westlake Village, CA 91362

Gauged graph papers for charting duplicate-stitching motifs available from:
Gail Selfridge
1509 Houston Street
Manhattan, KS 66502